John Paul II

The Man and the Century

We would like to thank the following people for their help with this book:
Marie, Annie Lemaire, Julian Ocaña, Teresa Rodriguez-Martinez,
Karine Balzer, Wilfried and Olaf Carstens
as well as Don Ruggieri and Mgr Fleischmann for their friendly support.

Translated from the French by Diana Wright

To a Slav pope the way is opened, the way to

the throne of thrones

This man will not flinch from the sword like that Italian!

This man, steadfast as God, will face the sword!

It is the world that is reduced to dust!

Crowds will draw strength from him and will follow

him towards the light where God dwells!

He will rid the wounds of the world of their vermin

He will clean the inner sanctum of churches and

sweep the threshold

He will shed a light on God as clear as day

Strength is needed to restore to God a world

that is his own

Here, then, he comes

The Slav pope, the peoples' brother

Juliusz Slowacki, Polish poet (1809-1849)

4

▲ On February 18, 1998, a young French girl named Marie gave John Paul II the first copy of this book, born of his untiring efforts for humankind. (Photograph Arturo Mari, with kind authorization from the Osservatore Romano.)

His Holiness John Paul II

On this Earth which He has allowed us to visit, there are and there have been many men and women who have known and know today that their life has value and meaning only insofar as it is a response to the question: Do you love? Do you love me?

These men and women have given and continue to give a complete and perfect reply – a heroic response – or even a common, everyday response. But whatever their reaction, they know that their life, that human life in general, has value and meaning only insofar as it is a response to the question "Do you love?". It is only by living with this question in mind that life becomes worth living.

Joannes Paulus PP. II

John Paul II

The Man and the Century

Marc-Eric Gervais

ELSA
EDITIONS

The Man and the Century

10 A New Pope is Elected

At the funeral of John Paul I.

Jesus said: "Follow me and I will make you fishers of men" (Mark 1: 4–17).

A New Pope is Elected

Ever since AD 67, when Jesus Christ chose Saint Linus as the successor to the apostle Peter, the election of a new pope has always been brought about by sombre news: "The pope is dead!" The pope's chamberlain, the camerlingo, certifies the death of the pope. He then summons the conclave, the assembly of cardinals who gather to elect the new pope.

▲ The death of John Paul I is officially announced.

Albino Luciano was born in 1912 at Canale d'Agordo. He taught theology and was ordained a priest in 1935; he became patriarch of Venice in 1969 and was made a cardinal in 1973. Following the death of Paul VI, the conclave gathered in the Sistine Chapel on August 25, 1978. After four ballots, Monsignor Luciani was elected. *"Tempesta magna est super me"* ("A violent storm is raging upon me") were the first words of the new Bishop of Rome, who took the name John Paul I. On September 27, the Pope summoned Monsignor Villot, the Secretary of State. He demanded the removal of Monsignor Marcinkus, whose name was linked to the Banco Ambrosiano scandal. A heated exchange took place between the two men. In the night of September 28, John Paul I died of a heart attack. He had been pope for only 33 days.

▲ John Paul I makes his first public appearance in the streets of Rome.

The conclave gathers in the Sistine Chapel. ▲

O n the eve of the gathering of the conclave that was to decide the successor
to John Paul I, workmen at the Vatican
had carefully closed all the exits and secured the
windows, making them fast with thick ropes.
Indeed, since the publication of the encyclical of
October 1, 1975, issued by Paul VI, the work of
the cardinals would be surrounded by the utmost
secrecy, the breaking of which would result in
excommunication. Thus, completely cut off from
the world for two days, the cardinals who were
gathered together in the Sistine Chapel were quite
unaware of the crowd that was waiting in St
Peter's Square in Rome. Down there, pressed
against the barriers that the carabinieri had
erected on Saturday morning, Pietro turned to
look at his wife and hitched up the shawl that had
slipped from her shoulders. Though deep in
prayer, Anna Maria interrupted her devotion to
smile at the man who for 30 years had been her
life's companion.

▲ The Crucifixion of St Peter.

▲ The Swiss Guard.

The Vatican City, the smallest state in the world, covers 109 acres.

It has a population of 800, consisting of clergymen and laypeople, who live there permanently in perfect harmony.

Links with the outside world are provided by a railway and a postal service. The Swiss Guard sees to the inhabitants' security. There are no taxes. The supermarket is often packed with customers; the Vatican prison, by contrast, is completely empty.

In AD 59, Peter, a fisherman, left Galilee and went to Rome, where he founded the Christian Church. Jesus had said to him: "Thou art Peter and upon this rock I will build my church; and the gates of hell shall not prevail against it" (Matthew 17: 18). St Peter is the first pope in the history of the Christian Church.

The Vatican is built over his tomb.

▲ St Peter's Square, Rome.

The Vatican spreads out around St Peter's Basilica. The construction of the basilica took place over 150 years, and 20 popes and 10 architects were involved. Since 1929, when the Lateran Treaty was drawn up, the Vatican has been an independent state which maintains diplomatic relations like other sovereign nations.

Another peculiar feature of this state is that the national feast day falls according to the date of the ordination of the pope.

14

▼ First appearance of John Paul I, August 26, 1978.

From that moment on, St Peter's Square was thronged with people. Night and day, nuns, pilgrims, believers or people who were simply curious were spontaneously united in the certainty of a faith which, only two weeks before, had been shaken. Everyone who now stood in that square, encircled by Bernini's double order of marble columns, wanted to consign to the past that black Friday in September when the world learnt of the sudden death of Pope John Paul I.

Everyone had felt a personal rapport with this ordinary man in the trappings of a prince, who had been elected within a single day on August 26, 1978, after four swift ballots. Anna Maria had wept. She, like him a native of Venice, had heaped upon the cardinals of the Curia responsibility for all the ills of the world. They had murdered him! The election of John Paul I, the smiling pope, had struck a blow for the meek and oppressed. Coming like them from a working-class background, he had quite simply been one of them. This pope, who spurned the papal tiara, spoke the people's language: "He was a great man and yet he knew how to be humble." But what did these Christian people know of the sufferings of Monsignor Luciani, the cardinal who, on his election to the papacy, had decided to take the name John Paul I?

When Monsignor Villot, the camerlingo of the Vatican, had approached him to ask him the ritual question "Do you accept your election?", the cardinal of Venice had been seriously tempted to refuse. He knew that he was ill. But in face of the crisis that was shaking the Church, he felt that he could not refuse. Christianity was going through an unprecedented crisis in the priesthood. The Christian Church, for whom humanity is a primary concern, was mired in financial scandals worthy of the detective novels of John le Carré. The word of God was being distorted by extremism. Worse, it was giving way to the advance of Marxism and was buckling under the financial dealings of the highly controversial Cardinal Marcinkus, who had been raised in America and in the shadow of the Mafia.

Very soon after his election, the Pope began to walk unsteadily. His brother Eduardo noticed that he was unwell from the time that he mounted the steps to the altar during the offertory. Dark circles often showed under his eyes. He held one hand to his chest and his face looked contorted. To his friends he confided: "I'm always smiling but inside, believe me, I'm suffering."

At prayer at 5 am on the morning after his election, he begged God to allow him to carry out his mission. Some people believed that he was crushed under the weight of his responsibilities. He was sensitive to a fault and condemned the dangers that threatened his Church.

From September 15, a list of some 20 *papabili* – potential candidates for the papacy – were circulated in a somewhat unsavoury manner in authorized circles. And yet the election of John Paul I was not what might be called a casting error. In 1972, he already had the support of Paul VI, who had made him Vice-President of the Italian Conference of Bishops. Acting in the full knowledge of these circumstances, the conclave chose a pope of whom much could be asked: he was the guardian of the principles laid out by Vatican Council II and the man who had emerged victorious from the fractricidal quarrel between the Italian cardinals Monsignor Siri and Monsignor Benelli.

▲ The future John Paul I, standing, centre.

Paul VI, whom Mother Teresa described as "a ray of the love of God in the darkness of the world", thanked John Paul I for his deeply felt humility and presented him with the ring of John XXIII, who was also known as "good Pope John".

15

▼ The funeral of John Paul I, held in St Peter's Basilica in Rome.

Pope John Paul I, himself feeling far from strong, knew that his reign would have to be strong.

Nevertheless, out of obedience to God, he had become pope. The people of Rome knew nothing of the problems within the Church and the internal quarrels that seemed to undermine relations between its ministers. Meanwhile, as St Peter's received the body of the "poor pope", killed by coronary thrombosis, the people of Rome were at a low ebb. Pietro Lombardo cried out against the injustice. In this country humiliated by corruption and shaken by the murderous attacks of the Red Brigades, the people sought a little humanity.

For these reasons, Pietro and Anna Maria were there to hear the name of the next Italian pope who would restore to their country a little of its greatness. ■

Keller / Sygma

At the heart of the election

In the secrecy of the Sistine Chapel, the conclave was aware of the feelings of bitterness that were running high in St Peter's Square. So long as the hand of God held back from designating the 264th pope in the history of Christianity, the business of the Church would remain at a standstill. Would the cardinals stay locked away in silence and individual prayer? Or, as with all political elections, would the balloting process lead to the formation of coalitions and promises of ministry? The fact that base haggling should be involved in the election of a pope ran counter to the ethics of the assembled company. But, for all that they were men of the cloth, these 1100 cardinals were also people of flesh and blood.

By the eighth ballot, Giuseppe Siri and Giovanni Benelli, archbishops of Genoa and Florence, knew that for them hope had faded. The election would be fought between the Italians and the foreigners. This was the moment that Monsignor Felici chose to lighten the tone among the assembly. Referring to the interview given by Monsignor Siri, which had appeared on the front page of the *Gazetta del Popolo*, he quoted the adage: "He who enters the conclave as a pope leaves it as a cardinal." When Monsignor Benelli failed to be elected at the next ballot, he mentioned the rumours that there would be an "r" in the name of the new pope. He recommended that Monsignor Benelli adopt the surname "Berelli" at the following ballot. Finally, savouring rumours implying that the pope would come from southern Italy, Felici would hum O sole mío every time he bumped into Monsignor Ursi, archbishop of Naples!

17

Meanwhile, and putting aside Monsignor Felici's jokes, electing a new pope was beginning to turn on a defining stake in the future of the universal Church. Who would be called upon to meet its aspirations? Who chosen to make of the Church a counterweight to change, as the youth of the world demanded? Would the reforms recommended by the Vatican Council II be put into practice or, precisely to the contrary, would the Church yield to the extremist ideas of such a man as Monsignor Lefèbvre? Two visions of the Church were in play. The "conservatives" rejected the forward-looking agenda of the Vatican Council II; the "modernists" were militating for the Church to follow an alternative path that had been underway since the 1960s. As early as 1959, Pope John XXIII laid the foundations of the Vatican Council II, the first meeting of which took place in the autumn of 1962. In four meetings held in 1965, 3000 bishops and others who attended published 16 schemata that defined Church policy for years to come. Vatican Council II addressed the opening up of the Church to the world, worked to set up a dialogue with other faiths, and instituted a collegiate Church shared by all bishops under the Pope's authority. It was amazing to see that, while the political world was caught off guard by the unrest of 1968, the Church had given thought to the development of society ten years ahead of time. Whereas governments were at a loss, the will of God would, in time, make sense of the contradictions of the rapidly evolving modern world.

For these reasons, God's representative on Earth had to be young and vigorous and travel the world to win over those who, quite simply, were not believers. The chosen one would speak to the poor, free prisoners and, according to the word of Jesus Christ, save the Church. So, as he had done with John Paul I, Monsignor Villot approached the Archbishop of Kraków, one Karol Wojtyla, who was set to become the darling of newspapers and television. The Vatican already knew him since he had been asked to deliver the course of 28 Lenten addresses during the annual retreat of the Curia in 1976.

The camerlingo leant over to Monsignor Wojtyla and asked: "Do you accept your election?" Karol Wojtyla looked at him intensely. Was he thinking of padre Albino Luciani, who dreamed only of carrying the Church forward on a wave of love? Was he thinking of his mother, Emilia Kaczorowska, whom he resembled and whose soul God had recalled to Him when Karol was still a boy? Two discreet tears rolled down his cheeks. Then, as though summoning up all his strength from these painful memories, he accepted God's choice: "For my lord Jesus Christ, for the Virgin Mary, out of respect for the apostolic constitution of Paul VI who invites him who will be chosen as our successor not to turn away from the duty to which he is called, I accept!" Monsignor Giuseppe Siri, Monsignor Giovanni Benelli and all the cardinals rose to their feet.

Spontaneously, the assembly broke into loud applause that continued for several minutes. Karol Josef Wojtyla, a Pole from Wadowice who had lost his mother at the age of nine, had been left for dead by the Nazis and had been persecuted for his faith by Stalin, marked the end of a succession of Italian popes that had persisted unbroken for four and a half centuries. From the very moment of his election, he had already stepped into legend. ∎

It was not until 1972 that the periodical *Time*, reporting on the ravages of drug-taking, forced the world to address this problem on an international scale.

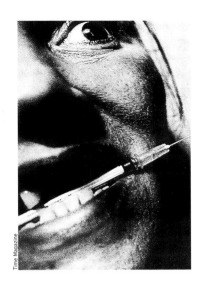

Time Magazine

In these late 20th-century times, the Pope has been criticized most notably for expressing his views on the domain of private life.

In 1968, youth rebelled against a repressive society. From Paris to Washington, young people protested and demonstrated against wars and oppressive regimes.

Gilles Caron

Yet, in 1978, much was expected of him. Today, John Paul II's position is generally considered to be too doctrinal but, although we want change, do we really know where we are going?

In 1978, how many fathers would have allowed their daughters to have sex when they had barely reached legal adulthood? How many unmarried women became pregnant and feared rejection by their families? How many of those women died because they could not speak about it?

And, these days, how many parents would still be upset to learn that their child were homosexual?

This clear-sighted pope was to work tirelessly to make us think about all these things.

19

▼ In 1970, Brigitte Bardot, wearing a nun's headdress, provoked a scandal.

CENSURÉ

Claude Azoulay

Even though God's guidance is sought when the cardinals cast their vote, the election of the pope is not a game of chance.

John Paul I and Karol Wojtyla, who took the name John Paul II, both played a very active part in current thinking about the evolution of the Church. The Curia and Paul VI paid close attention to their views, particularly during meetings of Vatican Council II.

▲ John Paul I in conversation with Monsignor Wojtyla, August 26, 1978.

▼ Paul VI and Monsignor Wojtyla.

At the time that Karol Wojtyla attended meetings of Vatican Council II, he already had a solid reputation, the establishment of which was significantly due to his published writings.

Paul VI valued him and John Paul I was in close agreement with his firm beliefs on the papacy's pastoral role.

Dagli Orti

▲ *L'Echelle de Jacob.* Musée du Petit Palais, Avignon.

Marc-Eric Gervais

His first words

As dusk fell, the last rays of the sun bathed the slumbering façade of St Peter's Basilica in an ochre glow. Suddenly, a great shout rang out over Rome: "Eccoci!" ("We've done it!"). From the chimney of the Sistine Chapel rose a column of white smoke that seemed even whiter against the darkening sky. The world was about to learn the result of the papal election! At this very moment, meanwhile, no-one doubted that, at a time when the third millennium seemed to have arrived more than a quarter of a century early, the name of the new pope would rock the Church to its foundations.

Hands joined or clasped in prayer, everyone was watching the loggia, where lights had just been switched on. Faces betrayed expressions of pride as television cameras turned this place into the centre of the world. The trumpets of the Swiss Guards rang out, proclaiming to one and all that the name of the next pope was about to be announced. As the figure of a man appeared on the balcony, an eerie silence fell on Rome.

Standing back a few yards, Monsignor Pericle Felici, wan-faced, scrutinized the crowd. In his capacity as senior cardinal-deacon, it fell to him to reveal the name of Saint Peter's successor. Such was the element of surprise that any error would be inadmissible. His job was to smooth the arrival of the "boss", the future Bishop of Rome. He took a deep breath and, with arms raised in a sign of victory, walked forward towards the crowd, a little nervous on account of the historic import of what he had to announce, and spoke the traditional words "Habemus Papam!" ("We have a pope!").

This was mere formality, and laughter was heard in the crowd. Impatient voices yelled "Chi è?"("Who is it?"). Things had got off to a bad start. Monsignor Felici, usually so articulate but troubled on this occasion, committed a historic lapse that only added to the crowd's incomprehension. He replied "His holiness Monsignor Carlum … er … Carolum Wojtyla." "Chi è?" By the flame of their cigarette lighters, some people were feverishly looking up and down the list of cardinals. Others were turning to those who beforehand had boasted of being in on God's secret. A woman's voice came to their rescue: "E il Polacco" ("It's the Pole!"). Instantly, the name of the new pope, intoned in all languages, babbled up from the crowd. Dumfounded, Pietro could not take in the news. Exasperated, Anna Maria spelled it out: "Si! Po-la-cco!" ("Yes. The Pole!").

Astounded, Pietro turned it over in his mind. "And why not Pavarotti in Swan Lake?" Monsignor Felici was at a loss to know what attitude to take.

Yet he insisted: "Wojtyla who has chosen the name John Paul II". Immediately, this evocation of the memory of the Archbishop of Venice provoked thunderous applause. In the shadows, the new Vicar of Christ had felt the mood of the crowd change from reticent to joyful, even though he had still to command that crowd's attention and, more crucially, win it over. At 7.15 pm, John Paul II came forward and appeared in the loggia of St Peter's.

His first words "Non abbiate paura!" ("Don't be afraid!") were greeted by an ovation. Bright eyes expressing his intelligence, the new pope went to work to conquer the crowd in St Peter's Square. "Praised be Jesus Christ!" he said and the esplanade erupted. After paying homage to John Paul I, the sovereign pontiff expressed to the faithful his deeply felt humility: "It was in fear that I accepted this election to office."

Anna Maria was swept off her feet by the spontaneity of a new pope who confided his feelings in this way. Even Pietro Lombardi began to feel at one with him, for he had also known fear – fear of unemployment, fear for his children's future. From then on, everything that the new pope said was greeted with wild enthusiasm. "I am trying to speak your language, our Italian language. If I make mistakes, you must put me right!" Unstoppable cheering greeted this confession, and at that moment Rome succumbed. It had taken Karol Wojtyla 32 years to rise through the Church hierarchy. As Pope John Paul II he had conquered the world in just three minutes.

Late that night, arm in arm on their balcony, Pietro and Anna Maria Lombardo felt serene as they contemplated the dome of St Peter's Basilica, which stood out emphatically against a sky dotted with thousands of stars. One star shone so brightly that the English tabloids emblazoned across three columns the headline "A Pope Star is Born." ∎

The Pope ushered in a new era. "Life is going to change. We will cancel debts and free slaves. Why? Because God will come among us. When? Today."

To Christians of modest means, the news of the election of a Polish pope, "the pope who came in from the cold", brought a real feeling of hope.

"*We had been told that he came from Poland. But, for me, here was a man who seemed to have left his fishing nets on the shores of some lake and, following in the footsteps of the apostle Peter, might have come straight from Galilee. Never had I felt so close to the Gospel.*"

André Frossart, 1982,
in conversation with John Paul II

While the people of Rome celebrated their first "Polish" night, John Paul II, "in love with God", as his friend Father Malinski jokingly put it, worked on his first apostolic blessing *Urbi et Orbi*. In the little chapel, he took stock of the task ahead. As the leader of his flock, he must strengthen the ranks and dissimulate this militant vision. So, for another night, each and every cardinal retired to his simple, bare cell and the Vatican refectory.

▼ Michelangelo's *Last Judgement*, the altarpiece of the Sistine Chapel.

26

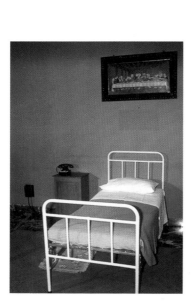

The next morning, in the Sistine Chapel, no trace remained of the election of the night before. The voting papers had been burned and the urn had been emptied of the ashes, signifying a return to the priorities of the spiritual world.

At 10.40 am, John Paul II delivered his first message *Urbi et Orbi*. On television screens, the victor of the night before seemed crushed by the weight of *The Last Judgement*, the fresco by Michelangelo. Grave and fragile, but adapting his manner of speech to the message that he wished to convey, John Paul II had already perfectly honed his image.

Speaking in a firm voice, the Pope set out his thinking on worship and prayer, the two main strands of a pastoral philosophy that he had been developing since 1946. He strongly reaffirmed the principles of the collegiate Church that had been spelled out by Vatican Council II. Then he quoted the example *wish* and *action*. This meant that all over the world the Church would never be indifferent to the suffering of humanity. Its philosophy was fundamentally based on religious and moral grounds.

John Paul II, elected at the age of 58, wanted to reinvigorate a lifeless Church. Taking a democratic approach, he called on the cardinals to go about their work even more enthusiastically. He begged them to help him in the great scheme for an ecumenical Church that he wanted to promote. The Pope, both as the humble child of the Virgin Mary and as "the rock of faith", assured his peers in the conclave that he would be their guide.

This was no empty promise for, like all believers and as the Catholic faith demands, he would remain true to his word. The promise was sealed with the words *"Totus tuus"* ("Totally yours"), a motto that he had adopted when he had first entered the Church. So impressed with his authority was the Curia that at the end of his address one of the cardinals remarked "This pope certainly has some surprises in store for us!"

At the end of these first two days, believers and atheists alike were hard put to keep up with the clichés that, in 20 years at the head of the Roman Catholic Church, the Pope would not succeed in throwing off. Everyone wanted the Pope to be an ordinary man like everyone else. But no-one had thought deeply about the profound reasons that had led him to accept his election to office. For believers, he would restore faith in an uncertain world. John Paul II had told them not to be ashamed of their faith. Yet, believers would be surprised to learn that in 1960 he had taken up a position in favour of sexual harmony. He encouraged couples "not to look on sexual relations solely as a means of procreation". In his work entitled *Love and Responsibility* he wrote: "Clearly, in love-making, the man must not be the only one to reach orgasm and this should occur not at the expense of the woman's pleasure but with her participation."

For non-believers, the Pope seemed a likeable man. He was going to inspire his lieutenants with ideas for change. All this did not take account of the fact that the Church is a pressure group that sticks to the words of the Bible, words from which the Pope cannot depart.

This pope held many surprises in store and even broke with the conventions of the times. He expressed his feelings from the balcony of the loggia. Humble in the extreme, he signed the telegram announcing his election thus: "Around 5.15 pm, John Paul II". In another show of spontaneity the day after his election, when he had forgotten to bless the staff of the Gemelli clinic, he was reminded of this little duty and joked "They're teaching me how to be the Pope!".

The press ran true to form. Headlines proliferated, labelling the Pope everything from "footballer" to "actor". To increase sales, newspapers invented outlandish headlines: "The Pope Was a Married Man!". This was the Gospel according to the *Illustrated Sport* or the Bible illustrated by the *Sunday Times*! John Paul II was up there with the stars. Popemania had broken out.

John Paul II presented himself to the world as a pastoral leader, and it was as a pastoral leader that he saw his role. But in the media madness that greeted his election, no-one registered the fact that the most important aspect of his words is the nature of his silence. The Pope inspires reflection, and this is what makes his commitment so forceful.

Fabian / Sygma

Through his silence, the affirmation of his love of God, the definition of his pastoral role, over the next two days, October 20 and 21, 1978, Pope John Paul II was to make plain the full extent of his skill in communication by stressing three words: collegiality, faith, and universality.

On Friday October 20, the atmosphere in the great hall of the Vatican consistory was formal. As they awaited the arrival of the new pope, diplomats huddled in small groups. On the dot of 11 o'clock, John Paul II made his entrance. In his role as head of the diplomats, Luis Valladares y Aycinema, the Guatemalan Ambassador, greeted the Pope. Responding warmly, the Pope set out his plans in the diplomatic field. He stressed the unbreakable rule of non-interference on the part of the Church; this underpins his attitude towards respect for the rights of the individual and, through the agency of the Church, he works towards relieving poverty and oppression, opening the eyes of the world to spiritual values and working with each nation

towards the greater common good. Having thus reassured the diplomats whom he had addressed, John Paul II stepped down from the rostrum to speak informally to each delegate in his own language. The ambassadors were captivated by the intimate manner in which the Vicar of God spoke to them. But, subtly, the Pope was exploiting the two aspects of his pastoral role. Dedicated to Jesus Christ, the Pope is the son of God and the son of man. As son of God, he is in charge of spiritual matters but, in his capacity as son of man, his task is to "relieve the sufferings of those whose dignity is compromised by hard times, neglect, selfishness or moral blindness." Blind to the fact that the son of man would intervene in the fullness of time, the ambassadors from the Eastern bloc would live to regret that day, they fell captive to his charm.

The next day, John Paul II completed his Herculean tasks by holding a reception for the international press in the great papal audience chamber. He was well aware that, after Paul VI's somewhat solemn pontificate, he must exploit to the full the modern communication methods that were beginning to be used by all those who wanted to be heard. Holding his audience in thrall, the new pope spoke with an arresting ease and stressed the importance of the quality of silence and reflection: "Let us spare a thought for the world in which we live." Speaking for several minutes, the new tenant of the Vatican established a parallel between his audience's common role in the diffusion of information and assured them that the Holy See would be open to any kind of sympathetic discussion. Then he gently warned his audience against the tendency of the press to generate hype and sensationalism. He reminded one and all that he considered journalism to be a type of ministry. For him, it was a sacred mission that consisted of reporting the truth. "Stay true to yourselves," he told them.

The very next day, the press was unanimous in proclaiming: "Pope John Paul II, a man of his time." ■

In 1978, the Holy Father invited everyone to think about the role of the press.

Did we heed him? In Colombia in 1985, a little girl called Omayra died as she sank into mud while photographers and cameramen recorded the event without going to her aid.

In the face of this most basic crime against humanity, we, like the Pope, question what kind of world we live in.

Speaking out publicly, the Pope strongly condemned this lack of compassion and stressed the obligations that people have towards one another.

This would be a constant theme of his reign as Pope.

The Holy See is a moral authority that from time to time forces the lay world to think.

Photographs Fournier / Contact

The Vatican exploits every modern means of communication.

Within a few hours of the outbreak of the Gulf War, John Paul II saw fit to accept from a young boy called Martin a game based on the Declaration of the Rights of Man.

The Holy Father, opposed to the war, appealed for peaceful negotiation.

Arturo Mari

Wolf / Explorer

The First Papal Mass

Gamma

Gamma

An enormous crowd had gathered on that Sunday, October 22, 1978. An estimated 300,000 people filled St Peter's Square and spilled out beyond Via della Conciliazione. Latecomers milled about on the lawns of Castel Sant'Angelo. A crowd the like of which had never been seen before had come to hear the Pope's first Papal Mass. Some people had waited for hours but for most their view of the altar was relayed via television monitors. Nevertheless, there was a joyful atmosphere. Working overtime, the street vendors that habitually exploited the Vatican tourist market had produced mementoes that were eagerly snapped up by the faithful of every nationality.

One by one, the cardinals come to kiss the Pope's ring. ▲

Poles in the crowd were beside themselves with joy. Slav songs mingled with the sound of African drums, a reminder of the contribution that the churches of the Third World had made towards the election of this "foreign" pope. To the right of the altar, royalty and heads of state were chatting quietly among themselves. Close by, the representatives of the non-Catholic churches admiringly watched a young Spanish woman with the face of a Madonna who, waving the flag of her country, was signalling loud and clear that the youth of the whole world was present at this celebration of faith. It was not unlike the Eurovision Song Contest. Then Mass began.

At 10 o'clock precisely, the cardinals, led by John Paul II, processed up to the altar. Despite the formality of the occasion, the crowd broke into deafening applause. Taken by surprise, the Pope stopped and, holding up the ceremony for a few seconds, turned to bless his fans with a friendly gesture. Quite spontaneously this unusual ritual, which from then on was to mark John Paul II's every public appearance, was established.

Meanwhile, the image that the cameras recorded was of a tense man who was feeling the weight of the cross that he had decided to bear. As he later admitted, at this moment he had recalled the

▲ Stole embroidered with the arms of St Peter.

▼ John Paul II and Monsignor Wyszynski.

serenity of a dying man who had whispered to him the words of Saint Paul: "I complete in the flesh what was missing in the passion of Christ."

Monsignor Wojtyla had accepted his election mindful of all those for whom God is still there when all other hope has gone.

Monsignor Pericle Felici walked up to the sovereign pontiff and handed him the pall that the sisters of the Benedictine monastery of St Cecilia had woven with wool from two lambs blessed on the feast day of St Agnes. Having declined to don the papal tiara, which for him was too heavily symbolic of the vanity of a Church that was all-powerful in the eyes of the world, John Paul II then received the obeisance of the cardinals.

The gathering was enthralled when Cardinal Wyszynski came up to kiss the Pope's ring. The Pope raised him to his feet and then kissed his hand. Watching the broadcast provided by RAI, the state-owned Italian television channel, Pietro Lombardo was moved and avoided meeting his wife's eyes. Once again, John Paul II had touched the hearts of the people.

Then the Pope rose to his feet to deliver his homily. Those political leaders who were present were treated to a strong lesson in religious conviction. Magnified by his investiture, speaking in a firm voice and fixing his audience with a bright gaze, the 264th pope in the history of Catholicism held one and a half billion television viewers by speaking simply of faith and of his belief in humanity.

The Pope's address, delivered in an assured tone, contained many echoes of the words of the Bible. Yet, for all that, this solemn homily was nonetheless a militant lecture. It was as if a general were rallying his troops: "Open wide the gateways to Christ, open frontiers between states, economic and political systems, the great domains of culture, of civilization, of development."

John Paul II blesses the crowd at the first Papal Mass of his pontificate.

thousands of young people were clamouring for him: reappearing at the window of his library, he gave them a last message: "You are the future of the world. The hope of the Church. You are my hope." Ending on a humorous note, he added: "We must stop now. It's lunchtime, for the Pope as well as for everyone else."

A few feet from the window, Zbigniew Brzezinski, representing the United States, looked on with pleasure. Now national security adviser in the Carter administration, he was thinking back to the occasion in 1976 when he had met the future pope. As a professor at Harvard, he had attended a conference given by Karol Wojtyla, then Archbishop of Kraków. So impressed was Brzezinski that he invited him to lunch. A personal correspondence then developed and continued even when he was called to Washington. Admiring the charisma of the Bishop of Rome, that American government official was convinced that here was a man who would change the world.

He went on: "Do not be afraid! Christ knows what is in your heart and only he knows it!" The look on the faces of certain ambassadors from the Eastern bloc expressed much about the warning that the Pope had just given them. To drive the message home, John Paul II began to speak in Polish. He begged his countrymen, from Jasna Gora and elsewhere: "I implore you to work with me. Never stop working with the pope." Carried along by a crowd that could not stop applauding him, he offered the Church the possibility of going there where it was not. Then he spoke in French, English, German, Portuguese, Spanish, Slovak, Lithuanian, and other languages. Embracing the world, he asked of it: "Pray for me, help me so that I may serve." In St Peter's Square, as in the hearts of people everywhere, lived the hope that a new and free man would perhaps change something in the state of nations. After an unscheduled walkabout, which greatly alarmed the security services, the Pope withdrew. Hundreds of

▲ Scene in the Polish countryside.

▲ Five scenes from the life of Christ. Musée du Louvre, Paris.

The Birth of a Vocation

Born on May 18, 1920 at Wadowice, a small country town in the Polish province of Galicia, Karol Wojtyla grew up in an epoch that knew hardship. He had plumbed the depths of human suffering, and this is what led Karol Wojtyla to his vocation: to work tirelessly for the good of men and women.

Dorothea Lange

Karol Wojtyla was a child of post-war Europe. At that time, victors and vanquished alike mourned their ten million dead and the mood of the times was summed up by the words "Never again". However, this was also a time of reckoning. The victors demanded from the vanquished crippling war reparations. The misery of the people and the absurdity of the speculators of Wall Street gave rise to totalitarian regimes: that of Mussolini in Italy, of Hirohito in Japan, and of Hitler in Germany. The future pope grew up in troubled times. He lost his mother at the age of nine, his brother at 12 and his father when he was only just 20. Humanity had on its conscience the 50 million dead of World War II. Karol Wojtyla chose the priesthood to care for the souls of men and women.

Gamma

▲ Karol Wojtyla at the time that he was secretly studying for the priesthood in Kraków in 1944.

Emilia Kaczorowska, the mother of Karol Jósef Wojtyla.

Gamma

n the square fronting the church in Wadowice, traders were setting out their stalls. The produce that they had to offer was meagre but, on that May morning in 1920, they breathed the spring air of freedom, a freedom that the Treaty of Versailles had secured for them two years previously. Emilia Wojtyla, née Kaczorowska, made her way carefully along paving stones that mist, wafting down from the Beskid mountains, had made particularly slippery. Her belly protruded. It would not be long before the wife of Karol Wojtyla, a lieutenant in the 12th infantry regiment, would give birth for the third time. Eight months before, at the first indications of pregnancy, she had been beside herself with joy at the good news. Normally so reserved, like all women of the time, she had leaped into her husband's arms. Together they had given thanks to the Lord for having in some measure relieved their sadness at the untimely loss of their little Olga six years earlier.

In 1920, Poland was made up of small country towns. The country's nascent industrial centres were based around Warsaw and Gdansk. Provinces such as Galicia were imbued with strong religious fervour.

▲ Pilgrimage at Kalwaria Zebrzydowska.

In 1925, the Polish state and the Roman Catholic Church signed a concordat granting Poland religious autonomy. Catholic religious education was given in schools. In church on Sundays, prayers were said for the Polish republic and the country's president.

Religious struggles – against the Russian Orthodox Church, the Prussian Lutheran Church and Austrian Catholicism – explain why Poles have fought fiercely for their freedom.

The Polish Church, like many clandestine movements, has a philosophy founded on rigorous principles.

Since the council of 1414, it has upheld liberty of conscience. Indeed, in Poland no-one was burned at the stake for their religious belief, and it was one of the few countries that refused to condone conversion to Christianity by force.

▼ Emilia Kaczorowska and Karol Jósef Wojtyla.

That child would live – for her, for them and for Edmond, their eldest son. So as not to relive the past, she wanted a boy. She would then have a second son. One would become a doctor, to care for people's physical needs, the other a priest, to care for their souls.

For now, she had to get back to 7 Koscielna Street. Edmond would soon be out of college. Twice Emilia paused for breath as she walked up the great stone staircase. Her shopping baskets hurt her hands and she felt the weight of the child, which uncomfortably filled her belly and kicked out in all directions. At last she reached the flat, and the front door that opened on to the kitchen. Although the Wojtylas were not well off, they were happy enough in their small two-room flat. Like the good housewife that she was, Emilia always made sure that her home was clean and tidy. Yet that day, May 18, 1920, she just had time to throw her shopping bags on the kitchen table, to sit down and decide, all alone, that the child that was about to be born would be named Karol, like his father.

A woman of hearth and home, Emilia devoted her time to her small son. Of course, Edmond was there but, now in his late teens, he spent a lot of time out of the house; he would arrive home later and later, having obviously enjoyed nights on the town. Meanwhile, the young Karol, nicknamed Lolek, opened his large brown eyes and stretched his arms up to his mother whenever she bent over the cradle, singing softly.

As Karol grew up, Emilia took a mediating position, tactfully standing between her husband and the boys. In a fragile Europe, where disturbing rumours were already circulating, Captain Wojtyla was determined that they should be raised to a strict regime. For him, the father, education was truly a question of ethics and of respect for national identity in a country that had successively fallen into the hands of the Russians, the Prussians and the Austrians. His great-grandfather, his grandfather and his father had grown up in a

"Germany has lost the war. Germany should pay." These words summed up the spirit of the Treaty of Versailles, signed in the Hall of Mirrors on June 28, 1919. The Catholic Austro-Hungarian Empire having been dismantled, the statehood of Poland and of Czechoslovakia was restored. The League of Nations (precursor of the United Nations) was set up to maintain peaceful relations and settle disputes between the different countries.

However, because it overlooked the reconstruction of Germany and had offered Poland the port of Dantzig, located in the middle of German territory, this peace treaty only served to bring out the bitterness of the German people who, 15 years later, fell in behind the process of revenge launched by a certain Adolf Hitler.

Ruined by the war and faced with the might of the United States of America, democratic Europe was not in a position of strength. Under the shadow of Communism, which overpowered Russia in 1917, political extremism was proliferating. In the Italy of 1919, Benito Mussolini was still only the leader of a paramilitary group in the employ of higher powers. But at the elections of 1921, the movement acquired 31 delegates. In July 1922, the Italian Fascist Party broke the general strike that had been declared by the opposition parties. On October 26, Mussolini unleashed his army, the Blackshirts, on Rome. King Victor Emmanuel III ceded power to him. Without even having engaged in battle, the dictator entered Rome like an emperor! From that point, the spectre of World War II was inexorably taking shape.

Imperial War Museum, London

BNF

Selling books door to door might seem harmless enough. But this was how, in 1920, Adolf Hitler began to spread his ideas. In the beer halls of Munich he sold pamphlets that were to form the substance of his book *Mein Kampf* ("My Struggle"). From 1920 to 1930, his ideas found a large audience among a population subjected to restrictions and to the occupation of industrial sites by the victors of World War I. Feeling themselves to be humiliated, a certain sector of the German people became increasingly receptive to the ideas of a man who spoke only of revenge.

41

National archives Washington

climate of resistance and of sacrifice, without which the Polish spirit would have broken under the yoke of these various foreign powers. Respect for dogma, which meant obedience to one's mother and father, and respect for people's inner conscience, was an essential characteristic of the education that Wojtyla, the officer, instilled in his sons. Of course, there were hard mornings when Lolek had to wash in icy water and, still shivering, set off to school on snow-covered roads, but he never complained. Edmond had gone off to university in Kraków to study medicine, and young Karol divided his time between primary school, where he excelled, and the life of the parish. More than the other little boys of his age he assiduously frequented the church of Our Lady, often going there with his mother. Very soon he was serving at the altar. He was also keen on football, and chose to be goalkeeper, the one who bites the dust while others stand tall. ■

▼ *St Joseph, the Carpenter*, by Georges de la Tour. Musée du Louvre, Paris.

42

Karol Wojtyla as a child.

His
First Troubles

Karol went on standing tall when, only nine years old and overwhelmed with grief, he had to live without Emilia's tender gaze constantly upon him. She had died of a kidney disorder. Thenceforth Karol Wojtyla was raised in a house deprived of his mother's gentle warmth; in spite of his father's devotion, he sought comfort in the arms of the Virgin Mary, just as Christ had done before him. In the mornings, on his way to school, he would stop at the church to pray. An altar boy, he served at Mass with a passion, unconsciously seeking to atone for a crime that he had not committed. He reproached himself for not having taken the time to love his mother enough. Karol was unhappy, but never showed it. In fact his friends stressed his enthusiasm and praised his kindness.

His father had stopped work and now devoted himself entirely to his son. He ran the house, taught the boy the principles of religion and stressed the importance of spiritual autonomy that had been granted by the Concordat of 1925. In a country at peace, father and son lived happily until that day in 1932 when they were plunged in mourning for Edmond, who died of typhus. Karol's brother had contracted the disease in the hospital where he was a young doctor. Karol was just 12 years old. Neighbours told how this second son went up to his father, who was crazed with grief. The child put his hand on the man's shoulder and with the utmost tenderness quietly said: "Courage, father. It is God's will."

43

On Thursday, October 24, 1929, share prices on the New York stock exchange plunged.

Since the end of the war, using funds raised through the sale of shares, the United States had provided aid to European countries and invested in their businesses.

But, aiming to bring down share prices only to reinvest while the market was low, speculators sold large quantities of shares.

Selling was too heavy. The money markets collapsed and the investors were ruined.

The United States cut off aid to Europe and withdrew its funds.

As a result, factories closed, unemployment rose, and poverty became widespread.

Then Hitler came to power.

44

G. Dutriac

Keystone

Bildarchiv Preussischer Kulturbesitz

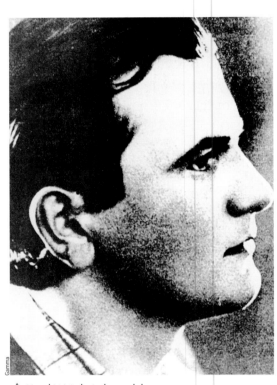

Gamma

▲ Karol Wojtyla in late adolescence.

Already the child was able to bring hope when others' hearts were too heavy to think of the future. Thus, Karol's gift was publicly revealed. With his father shut away inside his grief, the house no longer seemed alive. Plunged in the same silence, the young man fervently continued to serve at Mass. Little by little, religion became the recourse that allowed him to hide the extent of his own sorrows from others. In this way Karol Wojtyla spent his school years in Wadowice. His teachers described him as a youth who never made trouble, a good friend and an excellent pupil. He was passionately interested in all subjects, including philosophy, and enjoyed the company of others. He decided to join the theatre company of Professor Kotlarczyk, a teacher who greatly influenced him. During those years of rehearsals, Karol learnt about communal living, self-denial and control of emotion. Under Kotlarczyk's tutelage, he learnt how to project his voice, how to interpret a text and how to understand the origins of the events with which his generation was to be dramatically confronted.

Since 1928, Germany had been providing the National Socialist Party with an ever-increasing number of delegates. Karol was 13 years old when Marshal von Hindenburg's acknowledged political senility and western Europe's wanton blindness allowed Adolf Hitler to become chancellor in the most democratic fashion in the world. Soon afterwards, the wind of anti-Semitism was blowing through Europe and fanned the flames of hatred. But the Wojtylas clung to an evangelical faith. To those who expressed surprise when they saw Karol share moments of devotion in the church of Our Lady with his friend Jurek Kruger, son of the president of the Jewish community, the young parishioner replied: "We are all children of God." Wojtyla and Kruger were inseparable. Their friendship restored Captain Wojtyla's fortitude.

From then on he took the two boys under his wing, teaching and showing them many things, including aspects of Polish history and poetry. At the beginning of 1936, he looked fondly on the friendship that had developed between his son and a young Ashkenazi girl. Karol was very attached to Ginka who, two years his senior, could have been the older sister with whose memory he had grown up. When the first anti-Semitic persecutions in Poland intensified, this friendship became closer.

Marcin-Vadovius College was divided. Karol spoke up, pointing out to his fellow pupils that "anti-Semitism is non-Christian". His words had no effect. The pretty Ginka left for Palestine. Karol bade her farewell with a quotation from the Polish poet Adam Mickiewicz: "The Jew, our most ancient brother, hold him in high regard and help him on his way, for the sake of eternal well-being."

Having passed his high-school examinations, he went on to study philosophy and theology at Jagiellonian University in Kraków. In September 1938, while Europe, having feared that it would be shamed by war, was finding, in the words of Saint-Exupéry, that it would be "shamed by peace", the Wojtylas moved to Tyniecka Street, in the Italian quarter of Kraków.

Life was not easy, since they lived frugally on Captain Wojtyla's pension. Karol earned a little money by boiling up hot water for the workmen on a building site near their two-room basement. Daylight, which rarely penetrated these lodgings, was something that he sought out of doors. He met the poet Juliusz Kydrynski, and as a result was involved in the establishment of the theatre *Studio*. The great Nijinski was so impressed with Karol that he went as far as giving him a part in a musical comedy. But Karol the actor did not neglect spiritual matters and went on serving at Mass in Wawel Cathedral.

It was during the celebration of Mass on Friday, September 1, 1939 that he heard the terrifying thud of Nazi boots that were about to plunge Poland into a darkness from which it would emerge only 50 years later. ∎

Poland's darkest days

As the Luftwaffe screamed across Polish skies, marking them with its murderous madness, the young Karol, under order of Father Figlewicz, continued serving at the altar. The minute Mass was over, Karol set off for home, running across Kraków at breakneck speed. He ran faster and faster, despite the din of falling bombs, the cries of those who had fallen never to get up again, and the harrowing sight of children separated from their mothers. His father, desperately worried, was waiting for him in Tyniecka Street. Without a

Depardon

Bildarchiv Preussischer Kulturbesitz

Keystone

backward glance, father and son fled, carrying a small, hastily packed suitcase. For hours, with thousands of other refugees, they trudged slowly eastward. The group of walkers would dive for cover so as narrowly to escape the strafing of the Stukas of the Third Reich. As night fell, darkness blanketed the humiliation of a whole nation.

After an exhausting journey, having walked 125 miles, the group came to a halt. Russia had declared war on Poland and its troops had already taken Rzeszów. Karol and his father took stock of the situation. The destruction of the Russian Orthodox Church of St Saviour in Moscow, which had been ordered by the Kremlin in 1932, was still too fresh in their memory for them to confront the Russians. They turned back. Often along the way, Karol helped his father to walk and, in that tense night, every sound seemed a portent of danger. At last they reached Kraków. The city had been reduced to ruins; thick smoke slowly rose into the air and wafted away to nothing – like the freedom

that the Wojtylas had just lost. On September 6, Hitler's troops took control of their city. Two weeks later an exhausted Warsaw fell. In 30 days Poland had lost 20 years of independence, independence that had taken two centuries to secure. Worse, Poland had now to confront two tyrants: Stalin, who was annexing the eastern part of the country, and Hitler, who had designs on the rest. The madman of the Reich had sworn: "I will make of Poland an old forgotten name on the map of Europe."

The Führer had put Hans Franck in charge of Germany's Polish provinces. He was one of those heartless and ignorant officers from the days before 1933, whom Nazism, through its simplistic ideas about national ascendancy and slogans about the superiority of the German race, had quickly promoted. Hitler was relying on this older generation, frustrated men for whom the war presented an opportunity to restore a sense of their self-importance.

▲ Cartoon illustrating the German-Soviet pact of 1939.

From the autumn of 1939, the new master of Warsaw went about settling old scores with the city's defeated inhabitants: universities were closed, synagogues were destroyed, shrines were desecrated and people were deported on a massive scale. As an ultimate act of humiliation, a flag bearing the swastika fluttered over Wawel Cathedral. Systematically and rationally, to the measured pace of the goose–step, the destruction of Polish national identity was planned and carried out. Starting from an embryonic personal vision of the creation of a global economy, Hitler had decided that Poland would be a source of cheap labour for German industry. Accordingly, the only people deemed worthy of survival for the greater good of the Reich were workers and peasants. Those for whom there was no use – students, intellectuals, the middle classes, priests and Jews – were arrested, deported and executed.

Concentration camps were hastily constructed. Soon the Polish skyline was streaked with columns of black smoke rising from the ovens of the concentration camps at Treblinka, Auschwitz and Majdanek, which to this day put humankind to shame. If he were to escape persecution, Karol Wojtyla had no alternative but to offer himself for hire as a manual worker. Thanks to his strong build and determined demeanour, he was able to obtain an *Arbeitskarte* – the work permit that was a precious talisman against deportation. At the age of 20, Wojtyla began work in a quarry at Zabrówek that was owned by Solvay, the chemicals group. It was located no great distance from where he lived. The foreman was a Pole and the site was watched over by soldiers of the occupying forces. In temperatures that could exceed –86°F, Karol wielded a sledge-hammer and loaded broken stone into little wagons, which sometimes had to be carried, so deeply frozen were the rails. His fingers numb with cold, all feeling gone from his feet, his temples pinched against the bitter cold and jaw firmly set so as not to crack under the blows delivered by bored gangsters in search of amusement, the young romantic actor learnt to be resistant. Those Nazi ideologues had intended to break a man's spirit: instead, they made a pope of him. Poetic justice was also to make him the pope of human rights.

During this period, when his future was being shaped by this Polish landscape in the grip of an endless winter, Karol Wojtyla used his solitude and the hardship he was suffering to grow inexorably closer to God. Bent under the weight of his labours and gnawed by hunger, like his companions on the labour camp, "Lolek" was rediscovering the meaning of shared experience. Just like the early Christians, whose humanity was forged out of back-breaking toil, Karol treated persecution as an undertaking that had to be borne and the brutality that was meted out daily as a small sacrifice that proved his love of Christ. Blanketed by his faith, he leapt to the defence of his colleagues. He also saw to their religious needs, disregarding the fact that worship was strictly forbidden by Nazis, who would shoot for pleasure.

▲ Persecution of Jews in the Warsaw ghetto.

The invasion of Poland prompted Europe to declare war on Germany. Europe's military leaders heeded the words of warning given by Winston Churchill: "you had the choice between war and dishonour. You chose dishonour and you will have war…"

From 1939, wherever the Nazis had made inroads into Europe, people were arrested, deported, or forced to be "voluntary" workers.

What measures could the Nazis take against artistic expression, against the spontaneity of children whose impulse to be creative, to play and to love one another regardless of race was undimmed despite the bombings? What could Hitler have against love? As the V1 bombers combed the skies, Edna Brown, the great English dancer, set off to church to make her marriage vows to her fiancé, a pilot in the RAF.

▼ Detail from *Pietà with Donor and Saint* by Rogier van de Weyden. National Gallery, London

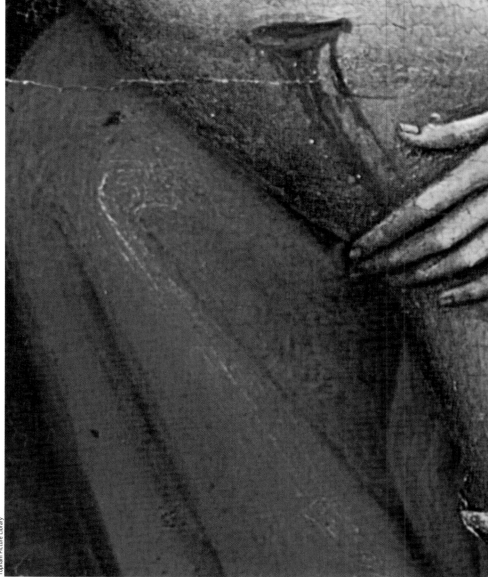

So it was that, risking his life, he went so far as to organize a Mass in memory of a colleague who died at his side. It was in his faith alone that this young man, 20 years old, found solace, for he could imagine no other calling.

Every night he returned home to his father, whom he fed and looked after: the woe that had befallen Poland had taken its toll on the older man. In the safety that darkness provided, Karol, condemned to forced labour by day, defied all-powerful Germany by night by burying himself in books and prayer. At dead of night on February 18, 1941, he prayed even more fervently than usual. In the late afternoon he had come home after another ordinary day of toil and humiliation to find his father's lifeless body. Captain Wojtyla, staff officer in the 12th infantry regiment, had finally laid down his arms. Entirely alone, Karol laid out his father's body, dropped to his knees beside the shrouded figure, and through prayer reached out to Jesus Christ. When the darkness of that lonely night gave way to the pale light of morning, Karol rose to his feet in the certain knowledge that he would enter the Church. Much later, when he had achieved greatness, those who heard him speak of distress and misery knew that he was speaking from personal experience.

It was then that Karol began a new life. A labourer by day, every night, with his friend the poet Juliusz Kydrynski, he cast off his chains. Defying the danger of deportation, the two accomplices gave readings from the works of St John of the Cross and put on informal productions of plays by Adam Mickiewicz. Just like those valiant Spanish republicans who, lacking weapons, went into combat reciting poems on the theme of freedom, Karol gave public performances for which he risked being denounced. While others went underground and took up arms, Karol Wojtyla's style of resistance followed another path. With his Slav temperament stamped with romanticism, he lit the darkness of that nonsensical night with the brightness of his faith.

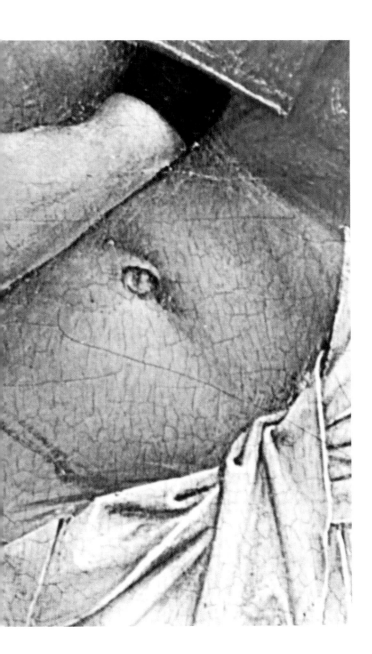

His faith lay in his country, in the superiority of the spoken word over barbaric orders, in the strength of humankind over those who had lost their humanity, in the value of his unshakeable belief compared to an ideology that he wanted to see banished. He had faith in life, such as he had had the night that he was hit by a truck driven by a Nazi. The officer did not stop. Knocked unconscious, Karol lay in the snow in temperatures below –60°F with his skull smashed in. Those who discovered him in the early hours of the morning thought he was dead. But his inextinguishable faith in God had carried him through and given him the will to live.

While travelling in a tram one day, he happened to meet his old teacher, Mr Kotlarczyk. Straight away he regrouped the company of adolescents from Wadowice who were passionate about the theatre. An actor as well an author, Karol, influenced by the Bible, threw himself into writing. He was behind the launch of a periodical that was outlawed by the Gestapo. Once free of the labour camp, he acted as its editor. In Poland, a country gutted by fire and running with blood, these young people risked their lives to publish a few pages of poetry. The very same risk had been taken by Federico García Lorca in Spain and by Paul Éluard, who had been locked away for having penned the simple words: "Freedom, I write your name…".

The Nazis would not and could not understand. They were powerless. Words cannot be shot down with bullets. From then on the name Wojtyla figured on the blacklist of dangerous terrorists and he was actively hunted. Karol had decided that, come what may, he would devote himself wholly to the cause even if that meant martyrdom. He would not betray his faith. It was in this spirit that he made a pilgrimage to the monastery at Jasna Góra and, in secret, prayed at length before a painting of the Virgin Mary known as the Black Madonna – the queen of Poland and the queen of all mothers. For four years he had led a double life. Tied to working by day, every night he stayed up to study for the priesthood until that Sunday evening when God came to his aid.

In his spotlessly polished boots, Hans Franck admired himself in the mirror at some length. What he saw was the image of a zealous executor of the final solution, grown chubby and tightly buttoned up in his SS uniform. However, he could not stop a grimace. He had a headache. The night before he had once again drunk himself into oblivion. Even raping terrified young peasants was no longer a distraction. The men from the Gestapo were on his tail. Back in Berlin, the Führer had flown into a violent rage. He wanted results and he was going

to get them! In spite of that splitting headache, Hans Franck whistled quietly to himself. This first Sunday in April 1944 would be a proud day for the Reich: he was going to put the boot in to some Poles.

The dreadful round-up began at dawn. The "ushers" of the Reich liked to catch their victims as they leaped out of bed. These liquidators of human bankruptcy, these trustees of an iniquitous justice delivered summons, without appeal, to every human being aged between 15 and 50 years old. Those who tried to escape were gunned down. Women who wept were beaten or raped, depending on their age. To the sound of machine guns, the shouts of the Gestapo and the howling of dogs, Kraków was thrown to the mercy of these dregs of humanity. On Tyniecka Street, the booted feet of an SS officer stopped at number 10…

While the Nazis beat down the doors with their clubs, Karol Wojtyla decided to distance himself from the world. He lay down on the floor, his arms folded in the form of a cross, and focused his

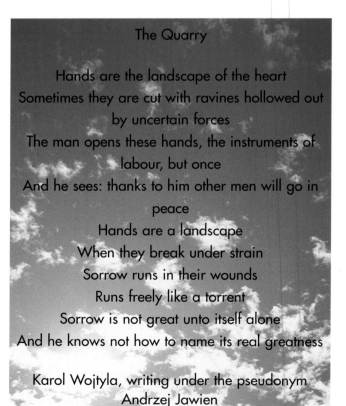

The Quarry

Hands are the landscape of the heart
Sometimes they are cut with ravines hollowed out
by uncertain forces
The man opens these hands, the instruments of
labour, but once
And he sees: thanks to him other men will go in
peace
Hands are a landscape
When they break under strain
Sorrow runs in their wounds
Runs freely like a torrent
Sorrow is not great unto itself alone
And he knows not how to name its real greatness

Karol Wojtyla, writing under the pseudonym
Andrzej Jawien

▲ *The Charnel House,* by Pablo Picasso, 1944. Museum of Modern Art, New York.

▲ *The Savant*, by Paul Klee.

54

thoughts on the compassion of the Virgin Mary. In the tumult – the cries of those who were condemned to die and the base laughter of those who were inflicting this suffering – "Lolek" shone like the small red light that in Catholic churches indicates the presence of the host. When the SS methodically searched every last corner, they overlooked that lowly basement flat: there, for the first time, a different light had begun to shine.

When silence returned, "through Christ, through the Virgin, my mother", Karol gave thanks to God and committed himself to God for life. For the last time and without a backward glance, he closed the door of his lodgings. In clear knowledge of what he was doing, he opened wide his door to God. Archbishop Sapieha welcomed Karol Wojtyla with pleasure: he had not been wrong that day in 1938 when he had detected in this young man of many talents a true religious fervour. Coming from an aristocratic family, Adam Sapieha was affectionately known as "the prince". He was appointed Archbishop of Kraków in 1925. Monsignor Sapieha did not have dealings with the occupying forces. He simply imposed his will. So it was that, lest his new seminarist be taken for a deserter, arrested and deported, he had Wojtyla's name removed from the list of workers at the Solvay factory. "Prince Sapieha" was concerned for the future of the Church and kept all his young charges in hiding in the cellar of the archbishop's palace.

A new episode in communal living began for Karol, and he apparently loved it. While the seminarists completed their training in the shadow of the denial of faith imposed by the occupying forces, Adam Sapieha, aged 78, carried out his duties without making any concession to circumstance. Monsignor Sapieha provided Jews with baptismal certificates and set up secret refuges for persecuted children. A rock of faith, Monsignor Sapieha was a role model for Karol. Someone with legendary status in Poland, the elderly man had one day taunted SS Hans Franck with the remark: "Even your Führer was baptized and, believe me, he'll need to have been." Prophetically, he added: "In the twilight of his days, despite the darkness of his soul, even he will carry out a last act of humanity." And so it was that, in the secrecy of his Bavarian bunker, before he escaped from the judgement of humankind, Hitler married his companion, Eva Braun.

On January 13, 1945, when for six months the music of Glenn Miller had entertained Allied troops all across Normandy, Stalin launched his greatest offensive against German forces stationed in Poland. A final battle took place. The two former allies vied with each other in their cruelty. When the machine guns finally fell silent, Poland, Karol Wojtyla's native country, mourned more than six million dead. Then, those who were still ignorant of the existence of the concentration camps came face to face with their full horror. As the doors of Sobibor, Treblinka and Auschwitz were opened, the depths to which humankind had sunk was revealed.

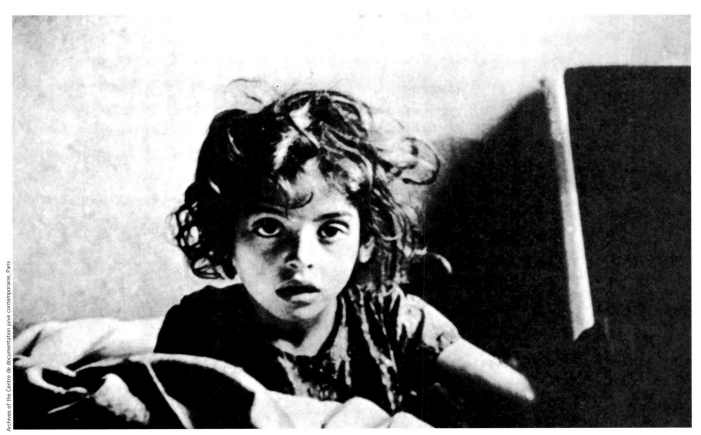

▲ A young victim of the concentration camps.

Everywhere, survivors were intoxicated with their new-found freedom. Yet at the same time, the guilty were hunted down. Worse, the unthinkable was being discovered. While the victors turned their thoughts to the post-war world, Hitler's suicide was coming to light and news of the dropping of atomic bombs on Hiroshima and Nagasaki was breaking. The war was over.

Humankind had been forever marked by these atrocities, committed in the name of humankind. A chapter in our history was drawing to a close. This chapter demands that we acknowledge the rare fortitude of a child of Auschwitz, whose only crime was to be Jewish.

A young man of just nine years old who could have been our child, he contributed to the defeat of those who despise human beings. At the entrance to the gas chambers, the little Halpern boy offered the Nazis a present that even they were not indecent enough to destroy. The gift was a drawing in which a bright sun shines out eternally over the black smoke of death. With this drawing the child lit up his final moments and our conscience for ever.

It was then that Karol Wojtyla irrevocably closed the door on this period of history, marked as it had been by the killer instinct, to concentrate on life. He decided to become a priest. ■

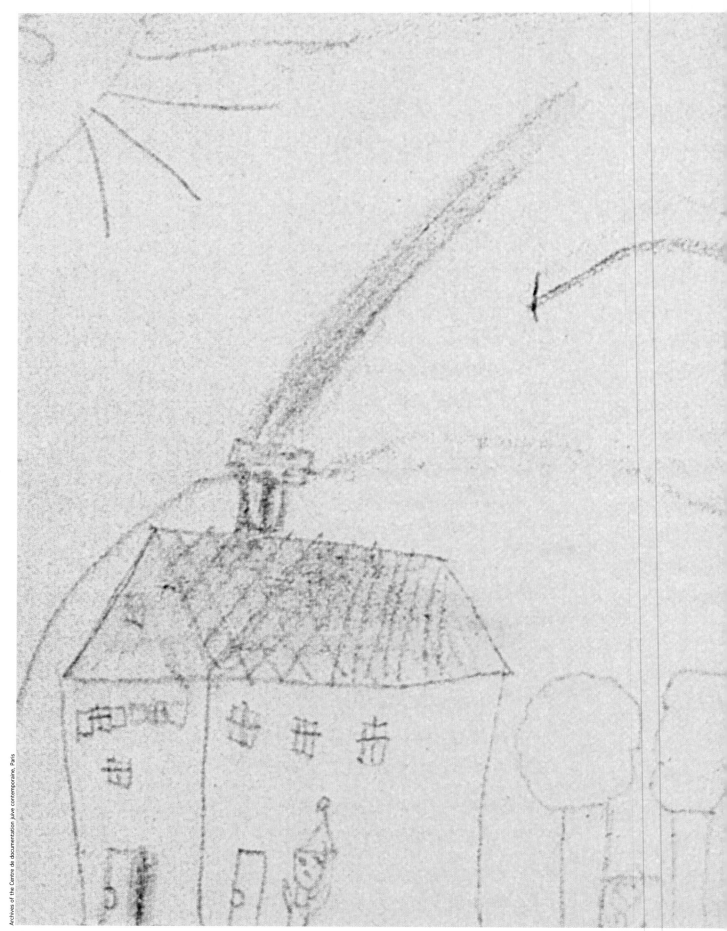

56

▲ George Halpern drew this picture for his mother, who was in hospital in France. This little boy, from Izieu, was deported to Auschwitz and gave the drawing to his executors.

Ambassador of Christ

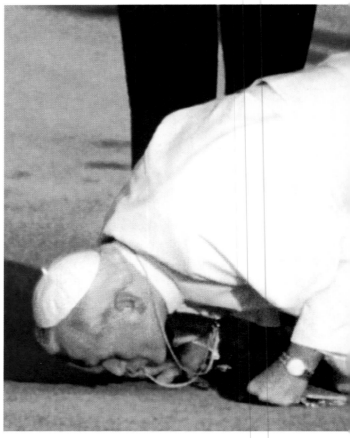

▲ On his arrival in Mexico, his first visit to that country, John Paul II kissed the ground. This gesture was to mark all his visits abroad.

From the moment of his election, the world keenly felt the need to invest all hope for the future in a new figurehead. The election of so remarkable a pope brought into focus the expectations of communities in need of change. Aware of this need, John Paul II immediately stamped his pontificate with the words of the gospel. More than a media star, he was the ambassador of Jesus Christ.

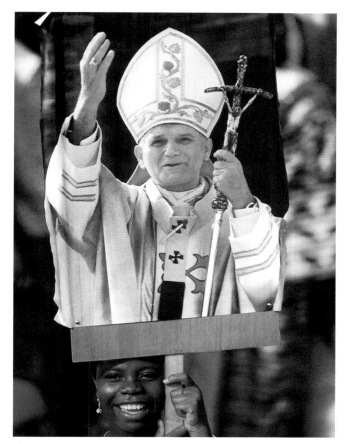

In Gabon, 1986.

Karol Wojtyla was ordained a priest in 1946 at
the age of 26, became Chair of Theology
at the University of Kraków at 34, was raised
to the bishopric at 38 and made Archbishop of
Kraków at 43. He was made a cardinal by Paul VI
on 9 July, 1967 and was elected pope on October
10, 1978. His rise was due to an unshakeable faith
combined with a progressive attitude towards
religious doctrine and a dogmatic approach to
religious practice. He stressed the bond between
religion and family life and the practice of daily
prayer. "The worship of Jesus Christ is not a part-
time occupation," he said. This pope would stand
as a figurehead for all those who sought a more
dynamic expression of their faith. He was also to
become the figurehead of the universal Church,
as, from early January 1979, would become clear
to the bishops of Latin America. Over 20 years,
the "supersonic pope" was to visit
every corner of the earth.

Wherever he goes, youthful enthusiasm greets the Pope.

Mexico, January 1979

A s the Boeing 727 began its descent through Mexico City's polluted skies on January 26, 1979, John Paul II, aboard the aircraft, gathered his thoughts. In an atmosphere of hostility, he was arriving to open the Third Latin American episcopal conference. In a country in which religion had been declared anti-constitutional since 1917, Catholicism was nevertheless fervently practised. John Paul II was not a man to dodge the issue. He was coming to restore hope to those thoroughly dispossessed and to re-focus a local Church that, grown weary of the sufferings of the people, sometimes employed the methods of revolutionary protest. Indeed, since the time of the episcopal conference held by Paul VI in Medellín in 1968, priests were developing the renowned "theology of liberation". In the context of the demands of dictatorial regimes, the attraction of armed conflict and the espousal of Marxist ideology grew ever more powerful among the Latin American clergy. But for John Paul II, who had had first-hand experience of communism for over 30 years, there was no future in taking that road. In Santo Domingo the previous day, he had clearly stated his position on religious doctrine: "True liberation is to proclaim Jesus Christ, free of all constraint, present in all men who are transformed, who have become new creatures." As he fastened his seat belt ready for landing, the pope smiled to himself. In Las Minas, a poor area, the message had hit home. When popular fervour had greeted his arrival with cries of "Juan Pablo, Juan Pablo!", he had persuaded the crowd to invoke not his own name but that of Jesus Christ.

A great clamour rose above the hubbub of the Mexico City suburbs. The pope's plane was coming to a standstill on the tarmac. As the hum of the engines died down, an extraordinary silence fell. Hundreds of photographers, zoom lenses at the ready, were poised to snap the Pope in a volley of clicks and flashes. As the doors of the aircraft swung open, the deafening peel of bells rang out from all the church towers in the land. President Lopez Portillo was furious. The sound of bells signalled the first set-back for a dictatorship whose constitution was one of the most anticlerical in the world. As the Bishop of Rome rose to his feet after having kissed Mexican soil, the country's premier stepped forward, his jaw clenched. Forgetting the watchful eyes of the media, he received the sovereign pontiff just as he would any emissary from Washington with a thunderous greeting: "Good day, Your Holiness!"

A few hundred yards away, while both sides exchanged formalities, Hugo Emilio Rodriguo Sanchez waited, deep in silent prayer. He wanted to catch sight of "Juan Pablo II". For three days, he had been waiting for this encounter that would last

▲ John Paul II and President Lopez Portillo.

61

but a fraction of a second. Though the heat of the sun was oppressive, he had removed his hat in readiness for the passage of the papal car. Little mattered to this agricultural labourer, like the 20 million others who had staked out the length of the papal procession. Their wrinkled hands and deeply lined faces betrayed a life devoid of hope. They possessed nothing. They had no rights. For them, personal freedom was a completely relative concept. All that mattered was whether there was food on the table, for themselves as well as for their children. For Hugo, that was no longer a concern. In less than ten years, life and the political climate of his country had deprived him of all his loved ones.

First there had been the earthquake of 1967, which had robbed the poorest of the little that they possessed. The Sanchez family had lost their youngest son: they had not been able to afford the medicine that would have saved him and he died

of cholera. A year later, it was the atrocity of the construction of the Aztec Stadium in which the World Cup was to be played. So as to avoid riots, which would in turn mean rehousing the destitute, the government had kept secret its plan to sweep away the shantytowns: without warning, the area was razed. One morning, Hugo and his wife had found Emilio, their third son, crushed in his sleep by the murderous navvies under the five pieces of sheet metal that had been their home.

The world turned a blind eye. The family's eldest son and youngest daughter went to see the padre: he did not have the heart to discourage them from joining the underground movement. Only too frequently had his sermons been interrupted by the crying of children that the local rubbish tip now only inadequately fed. Moreover, he was too often powerless to help tearful mothers who had lost their children. This priest to the poor felt keenly that he must be true to his faith. Just like Monsignor Camara, whose nickname was "the Che Guevara of the Church", certain clergymen were

actively subversive, occasionally even using firearms. Virile, fervent and fatally violent, this type of subversion was typical in South America. In essence, it was in complete contrast to the fight that Karol Wojtyla had fought against communism since 1946. However, this type of rebellion had been the only avenue open to Latin Americans. Eastern European churches, for their part, were supported by the democratic countries of the West, and notably by the United States. But South America was the Americans' back yard. In the secrecy of CIA Headquarters and eventually in the Oval Office of the White House, which governments were put into power and which destroyed was controlled by the CIA and dictated by US interests. What were the Sanchez children to do? There were only two alternatives: to go on suffering or to die for the cause of revolution.

It was eight weeks since the start of the World Cup, and words could not describe the grief that Hugo Sanchez felt. Military personnel had slain his son with a bullet in the back of the neck in the suburbs of Guadalajara. Rodrigo Sanchez had been murdered as, guilelessly, he daubed the wall of a stadium with anti-government slogans. He was barely 20 years old.

Four years later, on May 13, 1974, it was the turn of their daughter, María Asunción. Two police officers brought the news to Hugo and his wife. Arrested in Santiago de Chile, their only surviving child had not survived the questioning to which she was subjected by Pinochet's military forces. The young girl had been horribly tortured. A few days later, grief carried off Hugo's wife, Isabella. He found her lying down with her great dark eyes eternally fixed on the simple crucifix that had become her only hope.

For such people as Hugo Sanchez, the arrival of the Holy Father that morning of January 26, 1979 was practically a day of national liberation. His hands raised, "Juan Pablo" was unstoppable as he blessed this people, who once again breathed the sweet air of freedom. It was as if the whole of Latin America had turned out to greet him. The new pope slowly made his way towards the centre of Mexico City and, inexorably, into the heart of every Mexican. Nevertheless, despite the unparalleled warmth of this welcome and the sincerity of his smile, the Vicar of Christ was concerned. What he had to say to the fellow-members of his church, be they priests or padres, was uncompromising.

He knew that he was going to cause a lot of disillusionment. An opponent of Marxist dictatorship in Poland, he knew the importance of the role of priests and of faith. Fully aware of the tradition of violence in Latin America, he was determined that the Church remain the cornerstone of a fair society. Riding in the papal car, which was brought almost to a standstill so rapturous was popular fervour, the Pope was more than ever concerned... He could see these people. He was touching them. Their outstretched hands spoke to him of suffering and in their lined faces he read all the agonies that they had suffered.

For him, however, the love of God was immutable and it would never turn to violence. Even if everyone were to fight for the freedom of humankind, Jesus Christ would never be Che Guevara's comrade in arms. Naturally, the Pope also understood the impatience of his dispossessed people. His visit to Mexico had only one purpose: to make everyone, government ministers included, understand that the way ahead lay in a concerted effort so that they would no longer be "workers exploited and robbed of their rights, regimes that allow the exploitation of people by their fellow humans or by the state, that there would no longer be corruption, nor those who have everything in abundance while others want for everything through no fault of their own."

Meanwhile, as he was arriving at the nuncio's residence, where he was to spend the night, John Paul II had equally forthright words for President Portillo and the Mexican police force who, unseen, had cleared the papal route by their usual direct and effective methods. Next morning – for the Partido Revolucionario Institucional was powerless to stop the dawn of another day – the people of Mexico City awoke to their second day of celebration. Along the 12 miles of road that would lead the Holy Father to Our Lady of Guadalupe, thousands of people had once again turned out for him as if he were the Messiah. They had come directly from the airport and, so as not to lose their place on the roadside, had spent the night in the open air. Hugo, like many others in the crowd, was bleeding from his wounds. Driven by devotion, he had covered the last half mile or so up to the esplanade on his knees.

Hugo had been waiting for hours when shouts announced the arrival of the "padre". He wove from side to side to try to get a glimpse of him and suddenly here he was. It was better than he could have dreamed. As if by some miracle, the papal car

came to a halt right in front of him. The crowd lurched forward and Hugo was carried with it. Two soldiers, their faces masked by dark glasses, raised their machine guns but their fingers did not touch the trigger. The Pope had just taken the hands of this ordinary man in the crowd in his and was speaking to him.

The two men looked into one another's faces and as their eyes met Hugo found a look full of

compassion. The landless peasant who had lost everything, including his children, instinctively held his head high.

As though for the first time, Hugo felt as if he were an upstanding man and he dared to speak. For a few seconds he humbly told the Pope of his sufferings and of the fact that poor Mexicans were prevented from drawing attention to their plight. Just as he was to do later at Cuilapán with a Native American who came to speak to him on behalf of his family, the sovereign pontiff clasped this man to him. Then, with tears in his eyes, he continued to move along the remaining few yards that led up to sanctuary of the Black Madonna.

Moved by this impromptu encounter, John Paul II delivered one of the most moving homilies of his pontificate: "Build the Church." The new Bishop of Rome was addressing these words to his fellow clergymen. He was not only sending a message to those who were tempted by armed conflict, he was also imploring men of the cloth to join with those people, down there on the esplanade, who expected so much of him.

Then, standing before the Black Madonna, stressing the importance of the love that he wanted to restore to the world, he launched into a prayer to the Virgin Mary: "I repeat the words that are in so many hearts and on so many lips of the world. Hail Mary!"

Finally, elaborating on the dual sense of the "call to conscience", he intoned: "Live your lives as priests and servants of the Church. Do not work as company directors, political leaders or officials in a secular power." Twenty-four hours ahead of schedule, John Paul II had effectively opened the Third Latin American episcopal conference, which was to start in Puebla the next day.

In Puebla people had gathered in their hundreds of thousands, some smartly dressed for the occasion, others in rags, awaiting the arrival of Juan Pablo, whom they welcomed with shouts of "Viva el papa!" Hundreds of folk bands vied with the deafening sound of the bells that rung out from the town's 300 churches. Showered by fistfuls of confetti, John Paul II could make only very slow progress as he advanced towards the rostrum from which he was to open the conference. Then, in front of 128 bishops representing 22 countries, he delivered a magisterial, catechizing lecture.

In the old seminary of Palafox, the Pope's smile became set. He became implacable. "We must safeguard the purity of Christian doctrine," he stated. John Paul rejected the theory of a militant Christ.

"This idea of Jesus as a political activist, a revolutionary, as the dissident of Nazareth is completely at odds with the Church," he went on. Having dwelt for an hour on this theme, the Pope then turned his thoughts to humankind: "It is the duty of the Church to demand that thousands of human beings be given their freedom."

For the final part of his lecture, almost so as to put into practice what he had just expressed, the Pope went to Cuilapán. There he addressed the oppressed of the land. "Peasants who work by the sweat of their brow cannot take any more. Proper respect is their right. They have a right not be dispossessed of what they own, however meagre, by methods that sometimes come down to robbery or pillage pure and simple..."

His voice was firm and his sincerity unmistakable. On the parched earth of Cuilapán police officers could be seen falling to their knees and praying. Women held their children up and begged of him: "Don't go, Pablito."

But the Pope had to leave, to comfort other souls and fight other battles. And so, when his plane took to the skies, thousands of Mexicans held up mirrors towards the sky to signal their trust in him to show him that he had become their light. ∎

Eleven years later, in May 1990, John Paul II returned to a Mexico that had by now modified its constitution to legalize the Catholic Church. The Holy Father was welcomed by the people and by President Carlos Salinas de Gortari. The president even arranged for the Pope to meet a group of people working to alleviate the poverty that still gripped the country.

Hoffmann

▲ Atrocities committed at Auschwitz.

▲ An internee shows a US soldier the gas chambers.

Auschwitz
June 1979

Paralyzed by fear, the prisoner fell to his knees before the Lagerführer. He begged the commander of the concentration camp for mercy. As a reprisal for a successful escape, Fritsch had ordered the torture of ten wretched inmates of Block 14. Breaking ranks, a man stepped forwards, offering to take the place of this broken man. The Nazi officer asked him who he was to sacrifice himself in this way. "A Catholic priest," came the straightforward reply. With his fellow prisoners he was locked up in the starvation cell. His trial lasted 16 days, during which he was given neither food nor water. Then, on August 14, 1941, father Maximilien Kolbe breathed his last. On June 7, 1979, the man who, in his turn, walked down the corridors of Auschwitz was John Paul II.

He paused in front of the starvation cell, took a deep breath and, alone, entered the room, which was dimly lit by a window set high in the wall. John Paul II, the first pope in history to visit a death camp, knelt on the concrete floor on which his compatriot, and many others, died. He laid a spray of red and white carnations on the floor and prayed to honour the memory of those victims.

Despite the warmth of the Polish spring and fields covered in flowers, a shiver ran down the spine of those, outside the cell, who made up the Pope's entourage. Even the government representatives and the three ministers moved closer to the cardinals, who had come from Warsaw. Subconsciously Poland was recovering a sense of national unity. Sworn enemies since the end of World War II, communists and Catholics buried their differences and put behind them their battles to revive their common nationhood. Everyone present on that occasion felt that the Pope's visit was more than merely symbolic, a gesture on

which scorn might be poured in the years to come. In that little cell, Karol Wojtyla communed with his people. The Pope, once the Bishop of Kraków, was paying homage to mankind. He prayed for the parents of his dead friends. The Vicar of Christ showed a new dimension to his faith in humanity. The Cardinal of Kraków was mourning the six thousand Poles who had been exterminated in that Nazi night. As his lips touched Polish soil, John Paul II condemned all holocausts.

The Pope finally left the cell. He met the gaze of Stanislas Kania, a policy-maker of the Polish Communist Party, with responsibility for relations with the Church. The two men stared at one another, their eyes red with tears. Back in Warsaw, at the Ministry of Defence, Wojciech Jaruzelksi, sitting bolt upright in the corset that he always wore, was riveted to his television screen. Quite spontaneously, he crossed himself. This was the first time that the general, a fellow Pole, felt something in common with Karol Wojtyla.

At the very spot where the convoys of death had come to a halt, 200 priests who had survived the horrors of Auschwitz were awaiting the successor of the apostle Peter. A simple altar, made of rough planks of wood, had been set up and placed parallel with the railway tracks. On it was a cross surmounted by a crown made out of braided barbed wire. A piece of grey-and-white-striped material hung limply. It was marked with a number: 16670, Father Kolbe's number. John Paul II stopped to speak at some length to a group of women, survivors of the Ravensbrück camp. Then he stepped behind the altar. It was exactly 4 pm. Mass began.

John Paul II addressed the priests who were to say Mass with him: "Your robes are robes of blood." The silence was intense. Emotion rose to an intense pitch when he delivered his sermon: "I have often gone down into the death cell of Maximilien Kolbe. I have stood before the wall where executions took place and I have picked my way through the debris left by the ovens at Birkenau. As Pope, I had to come here. Now that I have become the successor of Peter, Christ wishes me to bear witness, before the whole world, to what it is that gives mankind greatness and reduces mankind to abject misery in our time. To bear witness to mankind's defeat and to mankind's victory. That is why I have come."

The Holy Father took it upon himself to speak in each of the native languages of the victims of Auschwitz: Polish, English, Bulgarian, Romany, Italian, Czech, Danish, French, Hebrew, Yiddish, Spanish, Dutch, Serbo-Croat, German, Norwegian, Romanian and Hungarian. The message was clear: John Paul II forgot no community. Referring to the sacrifice made by Father Kolbe, a Franciscan, he quoted his first papal encyclical, entitled *Redemptor Hominis* ("Redeemer of Man"), which had been published three months earlier. For the first time, a successor of Peter was addressing men and women of every social class and of every religion.

Religious authorities had pointed out that John Paul II glorified the individual, demanding that the dignity of the individual and the greatness of being human be respected. As the sun began to glow red as it sank down behind that sinister encampment, his words became even more explicit: "Is it enough to give a man a different uniform? To equip him with weapons of violence? Is it enough to impose upon him an ideology in which human rights are subjected to the laws of a particular system, totally subjected, to the point where they practically cease to exist at all?"

These words, charged with emotion, rose into the sky above Auschwitz. His voice betrayed a righteous anger and the crowd, which up until then had been meditative, burst into applause: this was both liberating and unexpected in this place. Commentators on Polish state television and many foreign journalists observed a long moment's silence. Some broadcasters could not hold back their tears. For the second time in 30 years, Auschwitz was cleansed of the hatred of humankind.

In that instant, the Pope's sincerity was obvious to all, especially when he spoke of the stele erected in memory of victims of the Holocaust: "I particularly want to stand, with you, before this inscription in Hebrew that awakens the memory of the people whose sons and daughters were condemned to total annihilation. The origins of this people go back to Abraham, our spiritual father. The very people who received from God the commandment 'Thou shalt not kill' were the people who, to an unparalleled degree, have known the meaning of killing. It is unthinkable that anyone could come before this inscription and not be moved." Then he paid homage to others, among them Edith Stein, a Jewish student who converted to Catholicism and became a nun and whom the beasts of Auschwitz condemned to death, like thousands of others. For this, John Paul II was accused of trying to

interweave Christianity with Judaism. The Pope, it was suggested, had reduced the tragedy of Auschwitz to the fate of a single converted Jew. People accused the Polish Church of secular anti-Semitism, quite forgetting that priests had laid down their lives to save anyone hounded by the Nazis. The assumption was that Rome, in taking over the symbolic focal point of the martyrdom of the Jews, wanted to gloss over Pius XII's ambiguous wartime position. The subject of the exodus of high-placed Nazis to Paraguay would be raised once again. The Pope was targeted by critics who voiced their disapproval of the establishment of a Carmelite convent within the gates of Auschwitz. These tactics were akin to those deployed against him when he was a priest in Kraków. He was accused of having Macchiavelian intentions. "This time, beyond a doubt, John Paul II has launched a takeover bid for Auschwitz." Throughout his reign the Pope was to live with these unfounded criticisms.

In reality, he had transcended the symbolism customarily given to this extermination camp. He felt the need to allow each individual to express his or her difference in this graveyard of the human conscience. Lest it be forgotten and for the benefit of future generations, he wanted Auschwitz to become a universal symbol of reflection and forgiveness. This place marked the climax of an anti-Semitic hatred that stretched back to time immemorial. But John Paul II made no distinction between victims, whether they were arrested for being communists, hounded for being homosexual, martyred for being Gypsies, systematically condemned for being mentally subnormal or executed simply because they were Jews.

At Auschwitz, as anywhere else where John Paul II was called on to defend human dignity, he refused to class people according to the colour of their skin, their religion, or the social class into which they were born.

This man, so widely criticized, worked tirelessly to uphold the sanctity of humankind. "You cannot be Christian and reject your fellow human." On that basis he was to be relentless in his condemnation of all holocausts and would lead his churches to repent for their failure to take action in the past. Last but not least, he would ask Christians to devote some thought to aspects of life that involve the exclusion of those who are different. Like it or not, this is the kind of man that John Paul II is. ■

▲ John Paul II with Mother Theresa.

74

▼ Mohandas Gandhi.

Assisi
October 1986

The idea had taken root in the mild Indian winter nine months earlier. In February 1986, John Paul II had met the Dalai Lama for the first time. Both men shared a similar sagacity, differing only in their respective religious faith. Both had experienced at first hand the spiritual fight against oppression. "To pray is to fight." When, in the course of his visit, the Pope paused before the tomb of Mohandas Gandhi, a victim of human violence, he secretly resolved to give to the world a Day of Peace. His plan was to bring together all religions, to honour the memory of Gandhi and thus to sanctify non-violence.

Belief in the power of faith to overcome the violence that people inflict on one another had long been at the forefront of John Paul II's philosophy. Cries of anguish of victims of the IRA were ringing on the streets of Belfast. Palestinian children were shot down by bullets from the guns of Israeli soldiers. Taken hostage, the citizens of Tel Aviv and of Jerusalem mourned their brothers and sisters, victims of suicide missions carried out by Palestinian factions. Almost as soon as the Baader-Meinhof gang had disintegrated, the Italian Red Brigades, whose agenda was to overthrow democracy, sprang up in its place.

Countless times the streets of Paris and its Métro network had been stained with blood. No-one felt safe any more. A few years later, even the impregnable United States was to experience terrorism, in the very heart of Manhattan. This was a world gone mad. Everywhere, words had lost their power and the only means of communication was through violence. This was a new era, and it demanded a new attitude. So it was that, ideologically several years ahead of the world of politics, John Paul II opened the debate in Assisi on October 27, 1986.

▲ John Paul II and the Dalai Lama.

The event had been planned along diplomatic lines. On April 13, 1986, the Pope had gone to the synagogue in Rome. No sovereign pontiff had ever taken such a step. The Pope and Rabbi Elio Toaff established a friendship that nullified a 2000-year-old religious rift. In the same spirit, that same year John Paul II had lent his full support to the construction of a mosque, the largest in Europe and the pride of the Muslim community in Italy. Unswayed by traditionalist factions within his Church, he even allowed the mosque to be built in the centre of the Eternal City. Respecting the plurality of faith, this ecumenical pope had simply applied the principles of Christian religion: "Love your neighbour as yourself."

Assisi, the native town of Saint Francis, the most pacifist and joyful of saints, was not a random choice of venue. However, at the time of the conference, world events were working against pacifism. A few days before, in Reykjavik, in the grip of the Icelandic winter, peace had been abruptly pushed out into the cold. The fact that President Reagan and President Gorbachev were manifestly at odds only accelerated the very arms race that the Assisi conference would endeavour to

▼ Chief Rabbi Elio Toaff welcomes John Paul II to the synagogue in Rome on April 13, 1986.

▲ John Paul II and Orthodox pope, Bartholomew I.

decelerate. As a prelude to this World Peace Day, John Paul II had appealed to all those involved in conflict throughout the world to observe a universal truce.

The Holy Father appealed to the goodwill of all people. This was a message for everyone, whether they be military personnel, heads of state or leaders of guerrilla groups. The Pope condemned killing: he wanted dialogue, even with "those who seek to attain their goals through violence and terrorism". In his soul, that of a Slav, he vowed to bring about the triumph of good through words alone. His show of strength was an entirely spiritual one.

As he stood in the nave of the church of Santa Maria degli Angeli, a smile spread across John Paul II's face. All were gathered here: Shintoists, Hindus, Muslims, Jews, Buddhists, Bahaists, Jains, Catholics, Protestants, Sikhs, African and Native American priests and even Zoroastrians. The faith of four billion people shone out through the joy of God's servants. Television cameras broadcast the image of this allegorical fresco.

77

The Holy Father rose to his feet. In a voice filled with love, he addressed his guests: "We shall not pray together. We shall be together to pray." The assembly stood. Each person prayed to his own god and for a long moment, the entire world was absorbed in meditation. There was resounding silence. Gunfire had ceased.

John Paul II spoke again: "If the world is to go on and if men and women are to survive in it, the world cannot do so without prayer." Tenzin Gyatso, the Dalai Lama, standing by his side, felt happy. As their eyes met, the Bishop of Rome smiled. He was thinking of the loneliness that his friend had experienced and of his exile from Tibet. They had in common the love of their respective native lands – countries stifled by the impenetrable darkness of totalitarianism. When the great powers fell silent, he would permanently restore a voice to those who had been silenced.

The afternoon was devoted to prayer and fasting. Members of the various religious sects dispersed in the places of worship in the town. Catholics were seen praying alongside their Muslim brothers. At the church of St Gregory, Native Americans smoked the pipe of peace with representatives of the Church in the United States. Although the atmosphere was one of contemplation, everyone eagerly awaited the final assembly for prayer that was to take place in a few hours' time in the square outside the basilica of St Francis. The town felt a sense of pride in being, for one day, at the centre of human endeavour. Waves of peace campaigners filled the narrow, winding streets of the old town. It could almost have been a scene on the banks of the Ganges. The world was cleansing itself. Mothers carried young children in their arms. Not for the world would they have missed this apotheosis.

As the sun set over the wide Umbrian plain, the outline of the Appenines was blurring in the dusky light. Representatives of the various religions were listening to the Pope's address. That morning, he had spoken about humanity: "This gathering today is an invitation to the world to become aware of another aspect of peace and of another method of obtaining it. Both will come from prayer." Now he was delivering another message to the fraternity

that he had gathered. "As religious leaders, you have not come here to attend an ecumenical peace conference, the purpose of which would be to hold talks or discuss universal strategies in support of a common cause."

Thus the Pope forestalled the idea of the establishment of a "League of United Religions". He respected the independence and unique nature of each system of belief: "This does not mean that religions can be reconciled on the basis of a common involvement in an earthly endeavour that would be greater than them all. Neither is this a concession to the relativism of religious belief, for everyone must honestly obey his or her conscience with the aim of seeking truth and of living in the light of truth…"

Night was falling on Assisi. When each religious group had recited its prayer for the greater good of humankind, John Paul II turned once more to face this gathering of holy men. In a measured voice, he announced the fact that on that day – October 27, 1986 – no gun had killed.

Looking up at the star-studded sky, everyone wondered how often in the 20th century a day had gone by when the cries of mothers who had lost their children were not heard or when lives had not been brutally curtailed.   ∎

▲ John Paul II in Benin in 1993.

▼ John Paul II in South Africa in 1995.

Christ Himself is African

In Ruhigi another day was dawning. This Rwandan village seemed to nestle safely in the verdant valleys of East Africa. But a truck had just drawn up on the edge of the settlement. Men armed with machetes jumped out. When they left, the ground was stained with the blood of the innocent people that they had just killed. Only a little boy of nine had managed to escape. He had slipped away from his hut and had hidden in a swampy ditch. His name was Mutolo Torimana, and when baptized he had been named Moses. Whether he was a Tutsi or a Hutu was immaterial. Now he was an orphan and he had just become another of the many victims of the killings that occurred every day in Rwanda.

When, on September 7, 1990, John Paul II arrived in Kigali to begin his seventh visit to Africa, he was painfully aware of the genocide that was raging in Rwanda. He had always paid particularly close attention to the events that afflicted the peoples of the African continent.

From the deserts of Morocco to the townships of South Africa, the Bishop of Rome had taken a special interest in Africa; this country was adrift, the victim of famine, AIDS, sexual violation, dictatorship and corruption; its natural resources were misappropriated and its people kept in a state of ignorance. A tireless missionary, John Paul II wanted to save souls and held that goal in his sights. On this continent, more than ever before, he would be the son of God and the son of humankind.

In Zaire in 1980, he had emphasized that "Christ himself is African". Naturally, like the apostle Paul, the Pope wanted to bring Christianity to peoples who may embrace other faiths. "Do not be afraid! Christ does not come to plunder but to save. He is here to give you life." In Kampala, the capital of Uganda, 13 years later, he stated: "May the word of God shine on your path and light your way."

Photographs Gamma

Beyond his perfectly understandable desire to spread the word of God, it was equally important to him to correct the imbalance that had resulted from the way in which the post-war world had been divided. On this continent, the pope who had come as preacher had become a militant for the fairer distribution of riches, the most precious among which would always be freedom.

In Senegal, on the quay from which people were once shipped as slaves to the Americas, John Paul II gave one of his most moving sermons in support of freedom: "Black people – men, women and children – were torn from their homeland, separated from their families, to be sold as if they were commodities. People who were baptized but who did not live according to their faith took part in this shameful trade. How can these human lives, crushed by slavery and disregard of the most basic human rights, be forgotten? This sin – committed by man against man, by man against God, must be confessed sincerely and with humility."

John Paul II unreservedly condemned anyone who sacrificed another for money. Not only was he referring to a period in history, he was also addressing those who today continue to withhold the keys of economic power. His role in the encouragement of dialogue between North and South – a role too often overlooked – was one of the marks of his pontificate. He even went as far as the United Nations International Court of Justice to demand greater social justice and press home the urgency of the programme that he wanted to see implemented.

Later, he urged Africans not to emulate societies that were dominated by materialism and the cult of the individual. He called on every individual to take responsibility for himself or herself and pointed out Africa's potential: "I am convinced that once it is allowed to run its own affairs, Africa will amaze the world with its progress but that it will also be capable of sharing its own wisdom." He also called attention to the

need to respect every human being with the words "Solidarity must replace selfishness." Meanwhile, on a continent where one person in four is a Catholic, John Paul II envisaged the development of the individual only in the context of respect for family values. From Tanzania to Nigeria, from Gabon to Equatorial Guinea, from Kenya to Togo or from Cameroon to the Democratic Republic of the Congo, the Holy Father's words concentrated on this theme.

If John Paul II wanted to awaken a sense of moral responsibility in the economic domain, he also wanted to champion a way of life that was in line with his thinking. Thus in Benin in 1982 the Pope ventured to speak of love: "Actions are like words that reveal what is in our hearts. Sexual acts are like words that show what is in our hearts." Many years later, he explained: "The language of sex demands commitment to lifelong fidelity."

Brushing aside words of caution, the Vicar of Christ upheld the Gospel against the custom of polygamy. He rejected adaptations of the words of the Gospel which certain members of the African Church, fearful that its faithful might turn to religions with a more permissive attitude, demanded. Despite the spread of Islam and the rise of religious sects, the Pope would countenance no departure from the words of Christ. For him, it was the only voice that would save these men, women and children of Africa, whose suffering he so intimately shared.

In Nigeria he spoke these magnificent words: "It is to the child endowed with human dignity and inalienable rights, to the babe in arms with the love of God reflected in his eyes and expressed in his smile, that I leave my message of fraternity, friendship and love." History will recognize John Paul II as one of those rare people who took an interest in the plight of each and every victim: whether a young person caught up in the ethnic strife of Rwanda or an Ethiopian suffering from rickets, a child of the arid Sahul or of the high plateaux, or a young Muslim girl whose life is circumscribed by her religion. John Paul II became "The voice of those who no longer have a voice." In this spirit he paid a historic visit to King Hussein II of Morocco that lasted several hours. On the occasion of the Pan-Arab Games in Casablanca in 1985, Hussein II expressed the wish that the Bishop of Rome hold talks with representatives of the 23 Arab Nations taking part in this event. Just as they had done three years before in Kaduna, Nigeria, Muslim religious leaders refused point blank to meet the Pope.

Yet, when he entered the stadium in Casablanca, 5000 young Moroccans gave him an overwhelming ovation, which became even more rapturous when he began to speak. "That a dialogue exists between Christians and Muslims is more important today than it has ever been," he said.

Ever respectful of the religious differences between individuals, the Holy Father called upon all to unite in prayer to relieve the ills of the world. But, besides his simple ecumenical wishes, John Paul II was disturbed by the rise of Islamic

Photographs Gamma

fundamentalism which, well ahead of others in this matter, he considered risked inflaming the world. He also expressed this fear to these young people. "We want everyone to reach divine truth in its fullest form but it is only in a climate of freedom of belief, unhampered by external constraints, that this can happen," he said. Spontaneously those young Moroccans rose to their feet and applauded at length this call for Islam to remain moderate.

The painful events experienced particularly acutely by the people of Egypt and of Algeria since the early 1990s prove that John Paul II's fears were, unfortunately, not unfounded. While the consensus among other countries was to adopt a policy of strict non-interference, the Bishop of Rome sought concrete solutions.

As soon as he was able, he appealed to large multinational companies to invest in these countries so as to bring real improvements to the welfare of the people and to support moderate

▲ This woman has just lost her eight children. This Algerian Madonna stands as a symbol of the 80,000 victims of the Algerian civil war.

AFP

Islamic governments so as to prevent extremism from taking hold. The Pope felt that the future of the third millennium depended on this, for he knew that religious fundamentalism fed on wretchedness and the hopelessness of deprived people.

All too few heeded his warning. Not a single major economic measure was taken to help these countries. Focused as it is on the money markets and on personal wealth, the Western world ignored the lot of those whom death visited daily. Then, in early 1998, the consequences of that lack of interest became all too clear when newspapers and television reported the atrocity that was visited on the Relizane area of Algeria. In the middle of Ramadan, about 100 attackers, under cover of assumed religious or military impunity, barbarically hacked 412 villagers to death. They cut throats, beheaded people and smashed the heads of babies against walls. What kind of human being is capable of committing such abominations?

On January 10, 1998, reacting to inertia on the part of other countries, John Paul II begged 166 ambassadors for some overdue action on the part of the countries that they represented. He told them, "I want to stress once again that no-one can kill in the name of God." Then, he ended by speaking of the various forms of violence of which the peoples of Africa and the Middle East are victim.In these parts of the world that are ravaged by hatred, a Palestinian man whose child had just been killed may be held up as an example. Carrying his child to an Israeli hospital, this man tearfully handed over the body of his only son. "May the death of my son save a child. No matter whether Arab or Jew so long as it saves a life." ■

Let morning
Shine on South Korea

hat day, May 6, 1984, the Pope stood before an enormous crowd. Their hands joined and their eyes closed, the citizens of Seoul stood as the South Korean national anthem was played. The final words of the anthem "The firm will, bonded with truth/Nest for the spirit of labour/Embracing the atmosphere of Mount Paet Ku/Will go forth to all the world" were greeted by loud cheering. In the crowd of thousands who had gathered in Yoedo Square, Yung Kim was praying particularly fervently. Like everyone else, he wanted to see the Pope and he had come to witness the beatification of 300 Korean martyrs, who died in the 18th century for having proclaimed their faith.

In Korea, John Paul II was issuing the decrees of multiple beatification that he had been granting since the beginning of his pontificate. In this country he had chosen to pay particular tribute to those unfortunate people who came from the humblest backgrounds. This was one of the ways in which he could give ordinary mortals a role model whose circumstances they could easily understand. The Pope had also wanted to include in this process the neighbours of these martyrs who had shown exemplary Christian charity by taking in their wives and children.

"Kohwang Manze!" As if they were at a rock concert, teenage girls on the verge of fainting were chanting "May the Pope live 10,000 years!" Dressed in traditional costume, they frantically waved the yellow flag of the Vatican City State with the armorial device of the Vatican City and the red and blue flags of South Korea that the authorities had distributed among them some hours before.

Some 12,500 miles from Rome, just as he was everywhere in the world, Jesus Christ was manifest. Standing in front of a vast cross, the Pope seemed small and frail. In his golden cassock, he looked like a flame that had come to light up the conscience of millions. "Equality of opportunity, by its very nature, precludes selfishness of any kind. Equality can only be reached through honest dealings." He condemned those industrial practices that, slaves to the demands of Wall Street, impose a new kind of serfdom in South East Asian countries. He firmly condemned the effects of the globalization of the economy that lead to the exploitation of the most vulnerable. "I pray that what you experience here will give you the conviction that only by speaking out and by making a firm commitment to human rights and values will the aspirations that lie in the hearts of all the peoples of the world be met." The Holy Father did not restrict his discussions to the issue of the martyrdom of Christians in Asia nor to the dramatic partition of Korea. He was drawing attention to the problem of those who are persecuted in the modern world. Crushed beneath the wheels of a system of subcontracting, millions of Asian workers survived on earnings of less than $18 a week. In this part of the world, where adults and children hire themselves out by the hour, he called for greater compassion, not to mention greater reason. He sincerely feared that uncontrolled growth and the rush to embrace materialism would impose on these peoples even greater hardship. The crisis in the Asian economy of the winter of 1997/1998 would, unhappily, prove him right.

In this country, where the first Catholic baptism took place in 1784, the Pope expressed his admiration for the Korean Church, a Church that "will be forever stained with blood". For John Paul II, the blood of martyrs was the seed from which Christians had sprung up. While a 1500-voice choir accompanied Holy Communion, administered by a thousand priests, television cameras immortalized the face of a teenage boy. Calm and contemplative, he showed no emotion.

Yet his history was as painful as that of his ancestors. Eight months before, on the night of August 30, 1983, a neighbour had roused him from his sleep to break to him the news of the Korean Airlines disaster. There followed a long night of anguish at Seoul airport. Yung Kim had learned that his parents would not return from so commonplace an activity as taking a flight. The Boeing on which they were travelling had strayed from its path by a mere few hundred yards. Officials at a Soviet military base had assumed that it was spying, and a Mig 25 cut short the lives of 259 passengers. The young Yung was also deeply moved when, at the end of saying Mass, Pope John Paul II drew attention to the necessity of creating a new kind of world. "When you try hard to make a better world, you need to keep your own life free of all contradiction. Your weapons are truth, justice, peace and faith: these are invincible weapons." ■

▲ In churches all over the world, altars remained lit so long as John Paul II remained in hospital.

▲ As a protest against the attempt on the life of John Paul II on May 13, 1981, people in working-class districts of Rome shut their houses up in silence.

Photographs Marc-Eric Gervais

The shooting of May 13, 1981

As teleprinters went into action, the news that they delivered was greeted with shock around the world. "The Pope's been shot." The bells of every cathedral began to ring out. The news spread at a phenomenal rate. As soon as they heard it, Christians hurried along to churches to light a candle. Believers and atheists were united by the same emotion. Thirty-five years earlier, the Nazis had wanted to crush him but they had made a pope of him. Poland was beginning to find its feet, and to nip this in the bud the Eastern bloc had tried to silence him. On May 13, 1981, for those who loved freedom, John Paul II was more than just a pope: he was becoming a legend!

That day, the Holy Father had lunched with Professor Lejeune, who had described to him a method of birth control that was acceptable to the Church. As he weighed up the advantages that this would bring to countries dogged by overpopulation, the Pope disregarded the recommendations of caution that the CIA had been at pains to impress on him for weeks. On April 23, William Casey, head of the CIA, had stressed that the situation was serious – the Pope was in danger.

For the past year, the Kremlin had been shaken by events in Poland. It had all begun with a railway workers' strike at Lublin. Edward Gierek, First Secretary of the Communist Party, was not alarmed: the strikes of 1956, 1970 and 1976 had easily been brought to an end. Wojciech Jaruzelski, Minister of National Defence, judged it unwise to intervene, since the country did not support this isolated movement. But, as John Paul II was preparing for the Feast of the Assumption at Castel Gandolfo on August 14, 1980, a worker shinned up a crane in the Lenin shipyard in Gdansk. Only that morning the director of the shipyard had notified Lech Walesa that he would be transferred as punishment for disobedience.

Founder of Solidarity, the trade union, this worker called for revolt and demanded that independent trade unions be made legal. Having had no response from Gierek, Walesa hardened his attitude. He demanded that censorship be lifted and political prisoners freed. In Rome, the Pope followed these developments on television. When, on August 21, the whole of Poland went on strike, John Paul II smiled wistfully as he breathed "At last!" Workers at prayer were caught on film. Photographs of the Pope and of the Black Madonna were tied to factory railings. The hand of God condemned communism. Even a cartoon showing that the Pope himself, in workman's overalls, with his arms folded, had downed tools was doing the rounds. When the workers began to express their discontent by singing religious and patriotic songs, Bishop Majdanski declared: "The seed sown by the Holy Father has taken root." Moscow could not afford to allow the corn of freedom to ripen.

Admittedly, since 1946, communist leaders had learnt to acknowledge this man, God's servant. While in the 1950s religious worship had been forbidden, Wojtyla had organized summer camps for young people. He played football, went trekking in the mountains and went canoeing. Religious instruction was never on the agenda, but sometimes, around the campfire, conversation would turn to the subject of freedom and the purpose for which humankind is on this Earth. Many a time Karol Wojtyla would tell students: "The police and the prisons don't cure anything. These methods only add to the price that will eventually have to be paid." When the government launched a religious movement intended to counter the Polish Church, Wojtyla responded by organizing a procession of the Black Madonna, which was paraded to every last corner of Poland. In 1979, when the icon had completed its tour of the country, millions gathered to follow the revered statue as it was taken back to the monastery of Jasna Gora. Karol Wojtyla was a thorn in the flesh of the Polish communists. As Pope, he was the stuff of Politburo nightmares.

On April 2, 1981, in Moscow, Brezhnev was even more beetle-browed than usual. He was mad with rage. Three days before, those "incompetent Poles" had managed to stave off another general strike only by negotiating terms with Solidarity. "Blood will be spilt," he raged, in front of his colleagues. "It's unavoidable. And if we're afraid of that we could well lose all that socialism has achieved." The Red Army took up position along the Polish borders.

In Rome, the Pope met the Soviet ambassador, who promised that his country would not invade Poland as long as there were no more strikes. John Paul II appealed to Poland for a mass return to work while Jaruzelski worked out a non-intervention agreement with the Soviet army in exchange for the setting up of martial law. At the end of April, Jaruzelski had to call on Monsignor Wyszynski's help to stave off another general strike. Moscow realized that Poland meant business. Brezhnev reached for the phone and called Bulgaria.

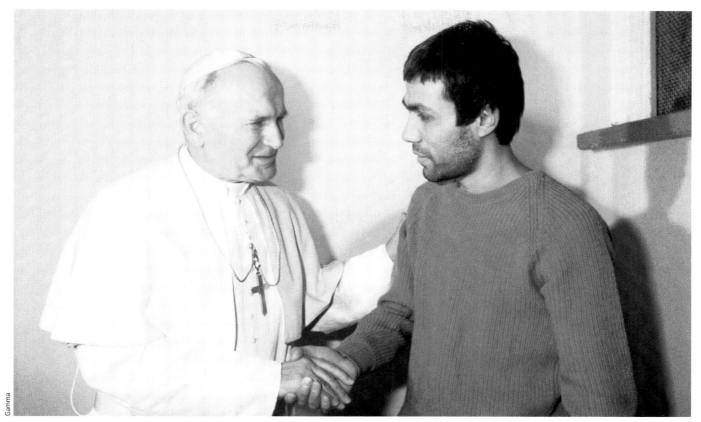
▲ The Pope visiting Mehmet Ali Agça, his would-be assassin, in his prison cell after he had been condemned to life imprisonment.

At 5 pm on Wednesday 13 May, 1981, the Holy Father was being driven round St Peter's Square in a white jeep. His secretary, Stanislas Dziwisz was at his side. The Pope was on good form. He blessed the crowd, propped up nuns who swooned in his presence, and kissed babies. It was business as usual for this "charmer of the faith".

In the crowd, Mehmet Ali Agça was waiting. He was not here to see the Pope but to carry out a contract killing. When the papal car passed slowly less than 20 feet away from him, he released the catch of his Browning 9mm automatic, held his breath and pulled the trigger. The pigeons of St Peter's Square scattered. Straight away, John Paul II staggered under the impact of the attack: he had been hit in the stomach and in the right elbow. As the wounded man was being driven to the nearest ambulance, police and the faithful surrounded the killer. Ali Agça did not try to run away. He was smiling. His mission had been accomplished, and being arrested was part of the plan. Every inch the professional, he would speak only incoherently so as to obscure the inquiry.

At the Gemelli clinic, the surgeon was becoming impatient. The Pope had a haemorrhage and he was at confession! Only when he was through could the surgeon operate. While he was on the operating table, almost 12 inches of intestine were removed from his abdomen and the anaesthetist accidentally broke one of his teeth. At 61, he needed a few days to recuperate before setting off on his next crusade.

Only John Paul II knows the truth: he went to see his attacker and spent some 20 minutes with him. At the end of this visit, Ali Agça, a Muslim condemned to life imprisonment, knelt down and kissed the Pope's hand. As a Christian, John Paul II granted the terrorist forgiveness and joined his mother in prayers. He will never betray the secret of the confession, and neither will he forget. With God's help and that of Ronald Reagan, Moscow was going to pay for the shooting of May 13. ■

Gamma

▲ On his first visit to the United States, John Paul II enjoyed hearing the talented Harlem choirs.

▼ John Paul II and Jimmy Carter.

Gamma

The Pope Conquers New York

He had been warned. But the Pope was still taken aback when he made his entrance to the Yankee Stadium on October 2, 1979. Cheering and applause shook the concrete building – home of the New York Yankees baseball team – to its foundations. Standing up in a white four-wheel-drive, his arms raised to acknowledge the crowd, John Paul II rejoiced. Before it had even pitched a ball, the Church of Rome had, in this country, just scored the most important home run in its history. That evening, John Paul II seemed to be blessed with the precision of Michael Jordan, the charm of John F. Kennedy, the physical presence of George Washington and the voice of Martin Luther King.

95

The moment that he had touched down in New York a few hours before, he had begun to conquer the most difficult city in the world. Before an immense crowd of people who had come en masse from Harlem, the black quarter, from the South Bronx, the Puerto Rican ghetto, and, of course, from Little Italy, John Paul II had scored a hit in a country that was financially so rich and socially so poor. It was on this theme that, for more than two hours, the Pope held in thrall sons and daughters of immigrants who, in their millions, ardently wanted the United States to be a country capable of sharing its riches, of redistributing wealth and financial security.

Over 14,000 journalists took note of his words: "The whole of humanity should think about the parable of the rich man and the beggar. Humanity should see it in terms of the economy and of human rights, in terms of relations between the former and the latter and the Third World." These words were received with an ovation the like of which Fifth Avenue had never known. According to the "clapometer", the Pope's performance easily outdid the parade of the crew of Apollo 11, even though they had gone higher than he did to conquer the Moon.

Beneath a gigantic American flag that flapped noisily in the wind, John Paul II was conquering New York, and beyond. "We cannot stand idly by while thousands of human beings die of hunger." He could not go on, so loud was the applause. In the most expensive avenue in the world, in the home of the luxury market, at the very heart of the symbol of the power of money, a Polish Catholic was making this appeal for generosity. Everyone, from the homeless of Madison Avenue to the yuppies of Wall Street, felt in their bones that the way had been opened for social dialogue to begin. In the eyes of the American middle class, proud of the Stars and Stripes, the Pope was erasing the hackneyed image of the United States as a self-centred country, a nation indifferent to the woes of mankind. Although the United States leads the world in raising funds for the benefit of charitable works, the view of America as a selfish nation was widely held. Many seemed not to recognize that generosity is in fact a tradition firmly anchored in American history.

The American people, inhabitants of this land of contrasts, were not merely flattered. Through their reaction to the words of the Holy Father, they were sending a clear message to Congress and to the White House that expressed desire for a social system worthy of the power of their country. The American people wanted an end to urban violence and to the drug problem, which were the root causes of the poverty and hopelessness that blighted towns and cities across the land. The Vicar of Christ ended his conquest of Western nations by inviting each and every person to realize their dignity as human beings. As the *New York Times* put it, the Pope had not only held in thrall 54 million Americans: he had captured the attention of the entire nation. That day saw the beginning of a political love affair between John Paul II and the United States which, in less than a decade, was to affect the future of the world.

The next day, John Paul II took the rostrum at the United Nations. Just as they had done for Pope Paul VI fourteen years before, the delegates politely rose to their feet to greet the Bishop of Rome. John Paul II immediately surprised his audience by starting with an apology. "Ladies and gentlemen, I apologise for speaking of things that, to you, must surely be obvious. However, it does not seem to me to be useless to speak of them, for what most often hampers human endeavour is that, in the achievement of that endeavour, one loses sight of the most obvious truths, the most elementary principles."

The delegates of the African countries were the first to break into applause. The diplomats had expected the "superstar" that the media had made of the Pope, but before them stood a man who spoke with humility. He appeared almost shy. His

▲ The Pope speaking at the United Nations International Court of Justice on October 2, 1979.

address was conventional. "Allow me to express the wish that the United Nations, by reason of its universal nature, should always be the forum, the high court in which the problems of mankind are evaluated in truth and justice." As the interpreters finished translating these final words, John Paul II turned to the subject of human rights and respect for life, themes that would mark his pontificate. He spoke out "against all forms of oppression or physical or mental torture inflicted by whatever system, wherever it is in the world." Delegates from one part of the world applauded; those from the other remained silent. The Pope expressed his concern for the future and identified the flash-points that lie like landmines all over the planet. He stressed the balance that mankind must achieve between the material and spiritual worlds. "Mankind lives in the world of material values and simultaneously in the world of spiritual values." The Pope called on those who possess wealth to share it with those who do not have enough to meet their most basic needs.

Of the Pope's first visit to the United States, some would remember his popular appeal or his words on morality. Others would be disappointed by his address at the United Nations. Few, however, would take note of a discerning insight, which was relevant for society everywhere: "So long as there is poverty in the world, the world will not have peace." The Pope was referring not only to conflict between different countries or to civil wars. He was giving poverty a quotidian definition, seeing it in terms of loneliness, lack of education, difficulty in making ends meet, alienation and unemployment. He was speaking of everyday poverty that, growing like a cancer in industrialized countries, would by the end of the century have overtaken many suburbs, too often making them no-go areas where boredom leads to delinquency and irritation to violence.   ■

▲ John Paul II and Ronald Reagan.

Gamma

Joining Forces Against Evil

Certain commentators felt that there was every reason to believe that John Paul II and Ronald Reagan would not hit it off together. On the one hand, here was a brilliant intellectual, and on the other a great fan of television game shows. According to the Vatican, when the Vicar of Christ felt like relaxing, he would meditate for hours on end. Washington was awash with satirical rumours: "The President spends his time trying to train a dog that flatly refuses to give him his paw. Reagan, however, has managed to shake hands with the dog…" The Pope extolled spiritual values; the former governor of California, by contrast, was all for liberalism. In fact, however, Ronald Reagan and John Paul II had many things in common.

Both had been actors and both loved sport. They knew the power of words to move crowds and they were united in their rejection of communism. So they met, they formed a personal alliance, they altered the course of history at the end of the 20th century and wrote the first chapters of the third millennium.

Well before Ronald Reagan was sworn in as president, John Paul II had secured important strategic connections with the White House. In fact, in 1976, he had formed a friendship with Zbigniew Brzezinski, a man of Polish extraction who had taught at Harvard and who had become national security adviser to Jimmy Carter.

At the end of 1980, American intelligence sources had good reason to believe that Soviet troops were about to be moved into Poland. The situation was delicate, and Jimmy Carter instructed Brzezinski to inform the Vatican. The adviser picked up the phone, dialled 00 39 66 982, identified himself to the Vatican switchboard and, as if this were nothing out of the ordinary, asked to speak to the Pope. After a few minutes' wait, allowing for the call to filter through at least a dozen Monsignori, Brzezinski got through to John Paul II: speaking in Polish, he explained to him the American government's position with regard to Solidarity. The adviser pointed out that Walesa's trade union movement received material help from American trade unions. He also revealed to the Holy Father that Jimmy Carter had authorized the CIA to infiltrate dissident nationalist movements in the Baltic states so as to weaken Moscow's position. Finally, he described in detail the movement of Soviet troops towards the Polish border. John Paul II thanked his caller and requested that he get in touch whenever he had anything new to report. Brzezinski then confided to the Holy Father that he had got through to him via the switchboard. To his great surprise, the American heard the Pope ask of his secretary, in all innocence, whether he had a personal telephone line. After a few seconds, Brzezinski was given the number of a direct line on which he could reach the Bishop of Rome.

A few hours later, Brzezinski needed to use that number to contact the Holy Father. Some satellite photographs had just been passed to him from the Oval Office. The Soviet army could clearly be seen within a stone's throw of Poland, putting up their tents and installing field hospitals. To this file was

Gamma

attached the report of a senior Polish officer whom the CIA had recruited two years back. Thanks to him, Washington was privy to the military orders that Moscow was giving to the forces of the Warsaw Pact. War was just round the corner.

The two men worked out an immediate plan of action. The Pope agreed that the bishops of those European countries with a large Catholic population would press their respective governments to threaten the Soviet Union with an embargo should it invade Poland. Simultaneously, President Carter was in touch with Brezhnev, appealing to him to consider the consequences of military intervention.

As to Ronald Reagan, he unhesitatingly reached for the phone and warned his future opposite number that he would become president within less than two weeks and from the moment that he was sworn in "the USSR will not find life very funny if it goes in to Poland". On that note, he hung up!

On January 20, 1981, Ronald Reagan took his presidential vows and became the 40th president in the history of the United States of America. Sitting for the first time in the Oval Office, he immediately asked to be informed of developments in Poland. Also – an extraordinary occurrence in the annals of the spoils system, by which all the members of the outgoing administration vacate the premises – Reagan brought Zbigniew Brzezinski into the White House as an adviser on Polish matters. Every day, William Casey, head of the CIA, and Richard Allen, national security adviser, would brief White House staff on the latest developments in American support for Solidarity.

At the end of this century, the CIA will celebrate its 50th anniversary. Throughout its history it has been the target of criticism from its detractors, who censure the organization for having known nothing about the fall of the Berlin Wall until the story appeared in newspapers. Yet history will pay tribute to the American secret service for its exceptional work in Poland. Through the CIA, the United States sent printing presses to Poland; it used its guile in secretly transferring to Poland millions of dollars; it spirited away agents whose lives were in danger; it infiltrated the Polish police force and the forces of the Warsaw Pact. These were the very ingredients of the spy novels of the decade.

Today, all this would indeed make a gripping read were it not for the fact that men and women had perished in that merciless and shady conflict. But, beyond a doubt, this was the price that had to be paid if communism in the Eastern bloc were to be stamped out, through the will of God and Ronald Reagan.

The son of an Irish Catholic father and a Protestant mother, Reagan had a working-class background. He had reached the top entirely through his own efforts and with the unfailing support of his wife Nancy. His life philosophy was founded solely on his belief in the virtue of

courage, in individual initiative and in the power of the United States. That is why, in his eyes, communism was the enemy that had to be destroyed.

Ever since the Yalta Conference of 1945, the USSR had challenged American supremacy. The two great powers were adept at destabilizing one another's respective zones of influence. The Soviets were arming South American freedom movements; the Americans, meanwhile, were providing funds to Eastern European countries to aid their political break-away from Moscow. Acutely sensitive to the Cuban situation, the Americans felt this effrontery to be a malignant cancer; the Soviets, for their part, considered West Berlin to be a shameful excrescence in the bosom of their empire.

The fight against communism was more than a power struggle – for the American people, enamoured as they were with the fundamental idea of freedom, it was above all a question of ethics. So that democracy should be upheld at the beginning of this century, the sons of Wyoming had fallen in the trenches of Verdun during World War I. So that mankind should not be slaves, their cousins from Dakota, Wyoming, Ohio and Wisconsin had come to offer themselves in sacrifice on the beaches of Normandy 28 years later. America knew its strength, and it had never failed when mankind was in danger. Thus it was precisely on this notion of fundamental freedom that President Reagan and John Paul II came to an agreement in that year, 1981.

But, for almost ten years, up to the fall of the Berlin Wall in November 1989, the reason for the association between these two men was seen simply as their profoundly anti-communist crusade. This feeling was widespread in those European countries that had only just thrown off the various dictatorships that had plagued them for so many years. In Portugal, on May 1, 1974, the "Carnation Revolution" led by António de Spinola saw the return of democracy. Then in July, having brought down the bloody regime of the colonels, Greece also reached the shores of freedom. In Spain, a year later, General Franco died. His designated successor, King Juan Carlos I, proceeded to set the country on the road to freedom.

But, shaken by the petrol crises of 1973 and 1979, Europe was also aware of its vulnerability. After 30 years of uninterrupted growth, it was with some surprise that Europe discovered the meaning of austerity and unemployment. European nations were looking for a change of leadership. New faces came on the scene. Andreas Papandreou, the socialist, and the actress Melina Mercouri in Greece; Alvaro Cunhal, the communist, and Mario Soares, the socialist, in Portugal; Felipe Gonzales in Spain or François Mitterrand in France fulfilled the wish for political change that was being expressed in Europe. Here were socialist and communist leaders with human faces. It was hoped that the smile on the face of such a man as Enrico Berlinguer in Italy would smooth away anxiety about tomorrow. Western Europe was trading with Eastern Europe. Colonies had been lost and new territories needed to be opened up. For these reasons, the war against communism waged by Reagan and the Pope was seen as a rearguard action.

Of course, progressive Europeans had read *Cancer Ward* and *The Gulag Archipelago*. They had been moved by the fate of the writer Alexander Solzhenitzyn and even publicly supported the physicist Andrei Sakharov, who was exiled to Gorky in January 1980. Conversely, they obstinately refused to believe first-hand accounts of life in Eastern European countries. These people, whom capitalism had condemned, found unbearable the thought that the only way forward should lead to an even more irreversible failure. Sensitive to public opinion, Western heads of state made a point of showing their independence with regard to Washington. Ronald Reagan and John

Paul II were alone in their opposition to the communist bloc. They had the presentiment that Solidarity was the Achilles heel of this colossus. Both thought that, should Moscow fail to stifle the Polish rebellion, it would be the shock wave that would send the Berlin Wall tumbling along with the regimes that sheltered behind it. The Pentagon and the CIA then went through a decisive period. Not since the Normandy landings of 1944 had the Americans engaged in such a psychological battle. In addition to logistical and financial support, Voice of America and Radio Free Europe broadcast non-stop news bulletins in Hungary, Poland, East Germany and Czechoslovakia. The American secret services played on the hatred of the Poles for the Russians and the deep animosity that existed between the Germans and the Russians. Several plans for popular insurrection were made. International financial organizations had been warned to give no more credit to Poland. The United States was preparing to cut its agricultural aid programme. Financially drained, the USSR would be unable to support Warsaw. In the spring of 1981, the dismantling of the Soviet empire was ready to begin.

But if it were to succeed, much more would be needed than lobbying the bishops of the Catholic countries of Europe. The cooperation of the European Community was essential. To kill off communism, Washington had to invert the balance of power as far as nuclear weapons were concerned; in this, the Soviets had so far had the upper hand. It was also necessary to sully the name of socialism in the eyes of European progressive thinkers. Jaruzelski's *coup d'état* in December 1982, the murder of Father Popielusko in October 1984 and Mikhail Gorbachev's surprising critique of the communist system when he came to power in 1985, when he unreservedly denounced the stultification of a society that had stagnated for 50 years, raised doubt in the hearts of committed socialists. The incalculable ecological catastrophe of the Aral Sea and the Chernobyl disaster of 1986 were enough to convince the most dogmatic believers. At the sight of pictures showing the desolation of Uzbekistan's great salt lake and those of the tragically inadequate methods being used to staunch radioactive leakage from the nuclear power station engulfed in flames, yesterday's partisans became fierce opponents of the Soviet system.

Finally, the White House had to persuade the Pope to be more than the son of mankind, that the situation demanded that he turn his attention to the secular matters of the world. In spite of the need to fight against this regime that despised his values, the Vicar of Christ showed himself extremely unwilling to embark on this course. It was at this point that Monsignor Krol made his entry in the history of the 20th century.

Jan Krol was of Polish extraction. His father had been born in a town not far from Wadowice. Monsignor Krol, now Archbishop of Philadelphia, was an exceptional man. He loved to smoke cigars, he had an unusual sense of humour and a very respectable swing on the golf course. To the delight of his friends, among whom was President Reagan, he never passed up the opportunity to bring all these qualities together.

Thus, one afternoon when he was playing a round on one of Washington's smartest golf courses, he caused such hilarity that the game stopped altogether. He was on the tee of the thirteenth hole at Augusta golf course known as Amen Corner, which for Monsignor Krol could not have been a happier coincidence. The flag was 190 yards to the left of the putting green, which ran alongside a small pond. Cigar between his teeth, Monsignor Krol gripped his number 5 iron and hit the ball as hard as he could. The ball rose up into the air, traced a gentle arc from right to left and, to an admiring commentary from the President, fell a few inches from the flag. The stroke had been almost perfect. But this was one of the East Coast's very quick greens; his ball stopped for only a fraction of a second and started to roll down the steep hill.

Slowing down, it passed within a hair's breadth of the hole then picked up speed, crossed the green and fell into the water. No-one dared speak. Taking a large puff at his Montechristo, Monsignor Krol ironically remarked: "And now you're going to ask me to believe in God!"

John Paul II liked this man, ten years his senior. In the 1960s they had studied for the cardinalship together. It was even said that, on more than one occasion, they were called to order in the refectory so rowdy did they become when they exchanged jokes from one end of the table to the other. When Monsignor Krol became a frequent visitor to the White House, dialogue with John Paul II became easier. But if Reagan was relying on the close friendship between Krol and John Paul II, the Pope was counting on his friend to influence American political stance with regard to South America. From that time, if anything was worrying the White House, John Paul II was told about it. Thousands of notes and hundreds of secrets were exchanged between the Vatican and Washington in the eight years of Reagan's presidency.

Such was John Paul II's influence that, four days after the attempt on his life in which he was wounded, President Reagan declared at the University of Notre Dame, in Indiana: "We will banish communism as if it were a sad and curious chapter in the history of mankind, the final pages of which are being written at this moment. It is Pope John Paul II that has sounded the alarm about these economic theories that justify injustice by invoking the rhetoric of the class struggle and by which, in the name of what passes for justice, a neighbour may be destroyed, killed, imprisoned or deprived of his most basic rights." If John Paul II had already earned the title "Viceroy of Ireland" when he went to Dublin in 1979, he was now indisputably on the way to being "the king of the Americas." In a country where marketing takes the place of spiritual values, he was turned into a star in the best Hollywood tradition. His face was painted on walls and drawn on pavements; it was

reproduced in all manner of ways and seen in the most unexpected places. John Paul II was not taken aback but instead used this cult to further just causes. Thus, each time he met emissaries from Washington or during interviews with American presidents, he would make a point of broaching the subject of the situation of the people of South America.

John Paul II had, of course, made a pact with the United States to fight against "the devil". Given his perspicacity, however, he did not only have Eastern Europe in his sights. The Vicar of Christ was too well travelled not to realize there were men and women in other parts of the world who were being badly treated by many a dictatorship. Naturally this was the motivation behind the position he had adopted with regard to Mexico and Chile.

Not all his efforts were understood. He was accused of supporting unspeakably cruel military regimes so as to stop the spread of Marxism. On

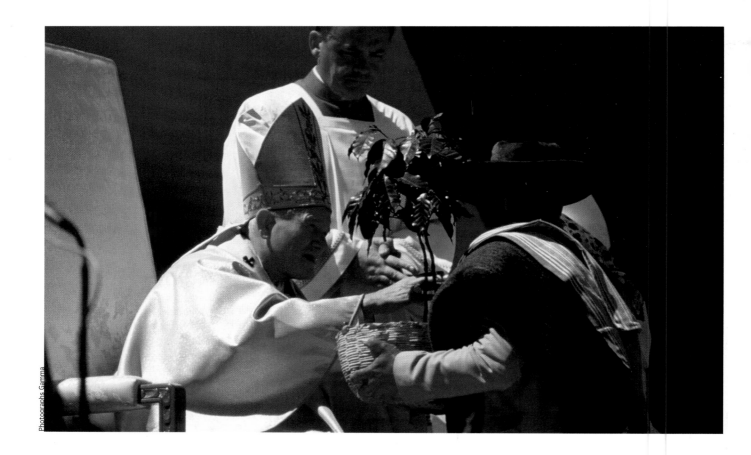

his visit to Salvador in March 1983, he was criticized for having mentioned only very briefly a certain Monsignor Romero, whom the military junta had murdered at the foot of the altar of his church.

His pontificate was in the dock when, in April 1987, he travelled to "Pinochet's Chile". Meanwhile, had anyone really listened to what he had to say? Had anyone really heard his call that war, injustice, suffering and death should cease? One day, in El Salvador, he had exclaimed: "Men and women of all creeds and political persuasions, listen to me: remember that every man is your brother: live your life as the respectful defender of his dignity. You can kill your brother slowly, day by day, when you deprive him of access to all that God has provided for the benefit of all men and not only for the benefit of a few." Five years later, in Santiago, before an astonished General Pinochet, he spoke these words, which were relayed by the international press: "Your dictatorship, Sir, is temporary."

It was not until his visit to Cuba in 1998 that the international press finally recognized that John Paul II was speaking out against all totalitarian regimes in South America. Naturally, some regretted the fact that he had chosen the option of slow and peaceful change rather than lend his support to action that could have resulted in swifter liberation for the people. Yet, whatever anyone's opinion on his approach to these problems, he could never be accused of not having been a dynamic ambassador for humankind. ∎

▲ Since 1959, Cubans have been forbidden to treat Christmas as a religious occasion.

▼ Fidel Castro in 1979.

Miracle in Havana

Tonight, Cuba celebrates Christmas! This was the headline which made waves around the world. John Paul II was due to come to Havana in three weeks' time, at the end of January 1998, and in anticipation of his visit Fidel Castro, for the first time since 1960, had given Cubans permission to celebrate the birth of Christ. Thinking back to the eight-hour speech that Castro had inflicted on everyone when he had paid tribute to "Che", even the Pope's most entrenched adversaries spared him a charitable thought: "Let's hope that Fidel doesn't start talking – John Paul really doesn't deserve that."

▲ In December 1997, traditional Nativity scenes reappeared in Cuba. For Cuban children, this was a novelty.

▼ In January 1998, Cubans found a new idol.

As he descended the steps of his plane, which had landed at José Martí Airport at 4 pm on January 21, 1998, the Holy Father was more anxious about surviving the heat than the loquacious habits of the great leader, whom he had already met in Rome in November 1996. At the aircraft door, he acknowledged with a slight wave of the hand the millions of Cuban Catholics who had turned out to greet him. At the bottom of the steps, the Vicar of Christ gently bent down to kiss the children of this island, the most isolated in the world. In the crowd, Osvaldo Serantes had a lump in his throat. Old *barbudo* that he was, he had been waiting for this moment for years. On December 2, 1956, he was not yet 30 when he had disembarked from the *Gramma* to liberate Cuba from Fulgencio Batista's corrupt regime. On the beach he had narrowly escaped being ambushed by government troops and had gone into hiding in the Sierra Maestra. Together with some 20 other survivors, he had even seen Fidel Castro at prayer.

Two years later, in 1959, millions of people, full of hope, had made their triumphant entry to Havana. With their bare hands, they had seen off the tyrant, who had boarded a flight to the United States on New Year's Eve. Osvaldo remembered the joy of the peasants when the land of which they had always dreamt was apportioned to them. Serantes sung along with these free men as they harvested the sugar cane. However, despite the indemnity made for American property-owners, the Cuban cause very soon ran into financial difficulties. Washington imposed a drastic ceiling on Cuban sugar imports and later followed this up with an embargo on the export of mechanical parts. Cuba was beleaguered. The country was about to collapse. Osvaldo Serantes thought back to the stormy debates that resulted in the government's expropriation of American interests in Havana. He remembered the reaction of fury among his comrades and of disbelief among priests, all of whom had supported the revolution, when Cuba, on its last legs, had fled into the arms of Big Brother – Soviet Russia. This marked the end of the romantic revolution. It was then that Osvaldo Serantes understood that socialism could never have a human face.

Nevertheless, he fought that tragic night in April 1961 in the Bay of Pigs when he had taken part in the repulse of the disembarkation of anti-Castro forces, armed by the CIA. He had even given thanks to John F. Kennedy, President of the United States, who like him was a Catholic, for having declined to provide the air support that they had requested and that would have allowed them to win.

Osvaldo had misgivings about Khrushchev's plans to install missiles in Cuba. He was not surprised when the next thing came along: land was divided up into collectives. Now he knew that his country was no more than a Soviet colony. But when José Martí Airport became the favourite port of call for airborne smugglers and when his country became expert at training the world's terrorists, Osvaldo

C.I.R.I.P. A. Gesgon

▲ Ernesto "Che" Guevara (1928–1967).

Serantes turned his back on his battle comrades and, notably, on his friend Ernesto Guevara, minister of industry

A medical doctor at the age of 25, Guevara was born into a middle-class family in Rosario. After having spent time in various Latin American countries, this Argentine joined the revolutionary army of Fidel Castro, whom he had met in Mexico in 1955. A political theorist who believed in permanent revolution, he held as an ideal the struggle against all forms of imperialism and the right to self-determination for all.

While, in 1965, Cuba was becoming a clone of Soviet Russia, Ernesto Guevara left the island and joined various guerrilla movements in Central America. He was captured and executed on October 10, 1967 by the Bolivian army. His real name has been forgotten, and he will forever be known as "Che". From the moment of his death he was to become a legend, not least because late

▲ John Paul II in Cuba in January 1998.

20th-century global marketing has had much to gain from using his name on a wide range of spin-offs marking the 30th anniversary of his execution. "Wake up, Ernesto. The world's gone mad!"

On January 21, 1988, at 4.07 pm, two men came face to face. A smile passed between them. Fidel Castro held out his arms and the Pope placed his hands on those of his host. Tomorrow's world had just been transformed. Two people – tired and ill – were coming together in impressive humility: a lesson for the world's political leaders. Bringing them together had, however, been no mean feat, so deeply rooted did their differences appear. This step had been more difficult for Castro since the stance taken by the United States in the 1950s had driven him to adopt the most intransigent dogma. In the twilight of his life, the Cuban leader had made an enormous effort to get to the roots of buried memories. Raised in the security of a Catholic home and educated in Catholic and Jesuit schools, he asked the forgiveness of his people and wished for absolution.

John Paul II was full of admiration for this man's self-sacrifice; he knew that putting an end to the economic blockade that had reduced his countrymen to a state of despair meant throwing himself open to judgement on the international stage. Hearing the heartfelt shouts of enthusiasm that rose up from this Cuban people, the Holy Father saw that both he and Castro shared an ideal for mankind – the ideal of liberation.

The portrait of Lenin that for 40 years had hung in a place of honour had been taken down. That Sunday, January 25, 1998, as John Paul II stood beneath a gigantic picture of Christ, Cuba had come to connect with quite another strand of history. Fidel Castro had promised it, and he was there. He wanted the Pope's visit to be a triumph, and it was.

Although he had invited his guest to speak freely, Castro was surprised when the Pope declared: "A modern state cannot replace atheism or religion with political idealism." But he rose to his feet to applaud when the Bishop of Rome denounced "neo-liberal capitalism that subordinates human beings to the blind forces of the market place". This was a condemnation of the US embargo that was afflicting Cuba. Half a million Cubans immediately began to chant "Free, free, the Pope wants us all to be free." Above the enthusiastic cheering, John Paul II replied: "Free, free, Cuba must be free." Even Fidel Castro allowed himself a smile.

This visit brought out the fact that religious belief was still vital, despite years of censure. Besides, the citizens of Havana had such a feeling of freedom that one journalist wrote: "John Paul II is now part of the universal heritage." But as John Paul II and Fidel Castro met each other's gaze, mutual respect, mutual understanding and an obvious desire to work towards the welfare of all could clearly be read in their eyes. In the 21st century, children will read of this decisive moment in the history of the world, when political ideology no longer kept people apart. ■

Photographs Marc-Eric Gervais

▲ 350,000 young people in the centre of Paris.

You are our Hope

Such ecstatic thanks for peace had not been heard in Paris since the city was liberated in 1944. United by a shared feeling of hope, a million young men and women were taking part in World Youth Day and together were winning the war against indifference.
To this cause these young people were dedicating a major global event of the late 20th century.

In the 20 years since he became Pope, John Paul II has covered seven times the distance between the Earth and the Moon. He has visited more than 140 countries and met at least as many heads of state, established new links with other churches, and strengthened the faith of millions of men and women. Thousands of times he has approached heads of state to plead for the alleviation of suffering and the restoration of universal human rights. His love of mankind has betrayed no empty promise. Let us think back to something that may be counted one of the marks of his ministry: the happiness of the German people as they trampled underfoot the Berlin Wall, which they themselves had helped to bring down. Whatever our personal creed, let us look at the faces of these young people on World Youth Day, and give thanks to the Pope for the worth of this undertaking, which has done so much to put the smile back on the face of a world that sometimes loses its reason.

▲ From Berlin to Paris, young people brought down the walls of shame, indifference and exclusion in exactly the same ways.

A festival of faith for young people.

Photographs Marc-Eric Gervais

As she boarded the underground train, Rosanne Marchand barely recognized the Métro. Everything was clean. The passengers were smiling. Even the windows had been cleaned. As she looked round for a seat, a young man gallantly got up and offered her his. She found herself sitting with a dozen or so Americans who had piled on to the train a few minutes before. They were singing religious songs, and others in the carriage were enjoying the performance. Parisians would normally be driven to distraction by such a din but, that day, August 19, 1997, there was no sign of irritation. Quite the opposite: an atmosphere of tolerance swept up and down the train, which had become a sort of cathedral. Since the day before, the arteries of the City of Light had throbbed to the rhythm of the extraordinary religious enthusiasm of a global youth. At the invitation of the Pope, girls and boys representing more than 160 countries had come from all points of the compass to celebrate the 12th in the series of World Youth Days.

Denver, Colorado, 1993. The Pope is in cowboy country, and the land where money is all. Despite the expense of getting there, 600,000 young people came to see the Pope. Much ink was spilled on the American Church's organization of the event. The prominent display of sponsors' names attracted criticism. Paris 1997 was to put this right; French companies preferred an effective message to an intrusive image.

Rome will be the venue for the first World Youth Day of the third millennium in mid summer of the year 2000. John Paul II had wanted it to take place in Jerusalem. Politics, unfortunately, move in mysterious ways. That an opportunity has been missed to bring millions of young people of every creed to a land that has known such a painful past is indeed regrettable.

World Youth Days were launched by John Paul II in 1985. The first of these celebrations of the Catholic faith took place in Rome and was attended by 250,000 people between the ages of 18 and 35. Buenos Aires was the venue in 1987. Next it was Spain, when in 1989 the ranks of the pilgrims swelled to 300,000 at Santiago de Compostela. One million attended the event in Poland in 1991, followed by 600,000 in Denver. In 1995, Manila, in the Philippines, saw the largest audience of any of the World Youth Days, with four million participants.

113

Grouped by nationality, they were put up in private houses, schools and convents in Paris and in the immediate vicinity. These "faith tourists" lit up the public transport that they used and added a splash of colour to the daily life of the suburbs. More importantly, they grasped the importance of this great international event of the late 20th century. In so doing, this group of people, several hundred million strong, gave the lie to the defeatist attitude taken by certain French newspapers, who predicted the certain failure of the Pope and the inevitable end of the Church in France.

In the carriage, a solitary, sublime voice suddenly began to intone "Many Rivers to Cross". The voice was so pure that everyone was immediately reduced to silence. As the music flowed, people tried to make out where this song was coming from. With her song, a young girl had transported these Parisians into the heart of African-American music. Although she was singing in the style of Mahalia Jackson, Nelly looked just like a typical California blonde. The music had shed its ethnic identity. With her eyes closed, a baseball cap worn back to front over her hair, she had the poise of youth. The sound of the blues was sweet. Opposite her, a young black man, with the broad shoulders

of the American footballer, flashed her a smile. A French girl who was a student nurse at the Necker Hospital spontaneously joined the group, joining this improvised performance of "Jesus Christ Superstar". Around her neck, the Hand of Fatima could sometimes be glimpsed. Noticing this Islamic symbol, Nelly, the American Catholic winked at Yasmine the French girl with Muslim parents. They were dancing side by side; by the end they had their arms round each others' waist. They were both ardent adherents to their respective faiths and proud of their respective origins. Rosanne was touched by this youth, which respected the differences it encountered as it celebrated the melding of East and West. At the same time, however, she could not prevent herself from thinking with sadness of a child who would have been their age.

The daughter of teachers, long-standing atheists, she inwardly reproached herself for having let herself be caught up in this charismatic ambience.

She buried herself in Monday's edition of *Libération*, where she read a news item on the World Youth Day under the explosive headline "Catholic Pride!"

Ostensibly this was a storm in a teacup. The headline was drawing a parallel between this event and Gay Pride. Every year, in springtime, in a colourful and exuberant festival the gay community parades through the streets of Paris to claim their right to be different. Although she was not a practising Catholic – like many other people, she had been baptized to please her grandmother – Rosanne did not find this parallel outrageous, even though some people had been shocked by it. The right of each individual to express his or her faith had been upheld with a touch of humour. In its own words, this daily newspaper was actually paying tribute to a youth culture that was far from shy about its creed and that took an open-hearted attitude towards a society that, it has to be said, no longer had faith in anything.

The group got off at Champs-de-Mars near the Eiffel Tower. Young people from other countries followed. Strains of Spanish and Korean intermingled with English and Italian; there were snatches of German, Swedish, Polish, and Lithuanian. The music of happiness filled the underground passageways of the Paris Métro. Surveying the scene from her seat by the window, Rosanne spotted Lebanese people proudly carrying the white flag with the cedar motif.

Suddenly a group of young Israelis stopped in front of them. One of the young men was waving the blue and white flag with the star of David. Smiles passed between them. To happy shouts, the sons and daughters of sworn enemies fell into each others' arms, as if to highlight the foolishness of the adult world's pitiful inability to stop wars. The train slowly pulled out of the station and rumbled away out of sight. The passengers seemed to be at peace. A few faces bore a new kind of serenity, buoyed up by this vision of hope for the future.

For once Rosanne finished work early, and she had a little time to herself. The children were away on holiday and her husband would not be back until late. She had been married for 15 years, and her spare time was usually taken up with looking after the family. Like that of millions of other mothers, Rosanne's life was compartmentalized, her time split between an increasingly stressful job and a domestic life that seemed less and less rewarding. Her week began early on Monday morning and ended in the late afternoon of Saturday, after the weekly visit to the supermarket. Altogether, it was a life that left little space in which to think.

Though she did not complain, this attractive 40-year-old was one of many who live with the constant worry of seeing their children grow up in a degraded environment. She wanted to leave the suburbs but she could not afford to. She worked for a company where taking a pay cut had been the only way to keep her job, and at the end of each month she was hard put to make ends meet. For some time, Rosanne had been wondering about the meaning of life. She was tired. She was ground down by worry about the future and the inability to believe in anything. And as two small tears began to well up, she automatically switched on the television.

Ettore Malanca

Marc-Eric Gervais

She was gripped by what she saw on the screen: Monsignor Sabbah and Monsignor Lustier were officiating at a service given in the open air. A homily, spoken in Arabic, was being given, and an unusual silence reigned. The Latin patriarch of Jerusalem was addressing the Christians of the Middle East. He called for the martyrs of Algeria not to be forgotten. His words were also intended for the North Africans now living in France. He was laying the ground for the message that the Pope was soon to give, against exclusion and against racism of any kind. At these words, 300,000 people, among which were tens of thousands of French people, leapt to their feet. In a spontaneous gesture of exuberance, berets and hats of all shapes were slung high into the sky.

The youth of the world applauded for many minutes. In a fraction of a second, under the happy gaze of Cardinal Lustiger, France rediscovered its dignity. How happy he was to see his country reborn in the eyes of these young people. World Youth Days had become an established event. The Pope had triumphed. Gripped by this moment of reconciliation, Rosanne settled comfortably in her sofa.

She like the sight of this crowd where united in equality, liberty and fraternity, people were as one. She wanted to believe in it. She liked the impudence of these young people, who were more adult than their parents. She could see that through sheer will-power it was possible to hope to change the world. Even so, she refused to feel guilty for having raised her children outside religion. Life left her barely enough time to teach them human dignity and respect for other people. She was envious of this crowd's unstoppable power to unite, she who often felt so alone. She gazed into the middle distance and the memory of a notice stuck up on the walls of Paris floated up: *Come and See*. In an automatic gesture that she had not made since the age of 13, she joined her hands together and started to pray. Later, she welcomed her husband home with a new-found serenity. She had made her decision. Whatever he might say, she would go and she would see. ∎

You Are Changing the World

Thursday, August 21, 1997. In the shadow of the Eiffel Tower, which seemed to rise incongruously above the peaceful atmosphere in the crowd of 500,000 pilgrims who were quietly gathering, the press centre was a hive of activity. The press team was efficiently fielding various questions that were being thrown at them by 3000 journalists. Now that the success of the World Youth Days was firmly established, new requests for press accreditation were flooding in from every corner of the globe.

That same morning, an Alitalia Airbus decorated with the arms of Vatican City had drawn up near the VIP lounge at Orly Airport in Paris. Under an already hot sun, President Jacques Chirac and his wife were waiting for the Pope to leave the aircraft. France's first lady, wearing a black veil, was visibly moved. At 10.27, the aircraft's heavy forward door swung open and an elderly man stepped out: he was stooped but then stood upright as he smiled. He acknowledged his hosts then walked down the steps and along the first few yards of the French Republic's red carpet. Under the watchful eyes of the governors of the most atheist country in Europe, John Paul II began his seventh visit to France.

Jacques Chirac wanted to bow before the Vicar of Christ but he kept to a handshake. A row was already erupting on the importance that the media were giving the Pope's visit. That was the reason why the French president had been advised to go against his personal convictions. It was thus as head of state, respectful of the creeds of all French people, that the most senior person in government stepped forward to greet the Holy Father.

This visit gave John Paul II the opportunity compare the styles of the different occupants of the presidential palace. On May 31, 1980, The Pope's visit to President Giscard d'Estaing had turned into a nightmare. Parisian society had practically fought to the death for the opportunity to meet the new Bishop of Rome. The President of the French Republic had personally helped the wives of government ministers to hoist themselves in through the palace windows in order to take refuge there. Very many of them, mad with rage, hurriedly had to leave the premises when their skirts, tights or undergarments had not stood up to this challenging "rise to power". President Mitterrand had neatly side stepped the problem. He quite simply baulked at receiving the Pope in Paris. No matter: the Pope was triumphantly welcomed outside the capital. Organizing the Pope's time in Paris, Jacques Chirac had opted for a schedule

▲ John Paul II and Jacques Chirac, President of France.

devoid of any ceremony that might tire him out. On the steps of the Élysée Palace, the two men had briefly turned to face the photographers. Very tactfully and very respectfully, the president measured his pace and moulded his attitude to that of his guest.

At 11.30 am, Jacques Chirac began his short speech. At certain times, he seemed to express real humanist intentions. The president spoke of the state's responsibility for society's moral decline. He drew lessons from history, as he did in May 1995 when he became the first French head of state to acknowledge that France must share the blame for the persecution of the Jews during World War II. He finished with these words: "Holy Father, you are a guide, a point of reference."

John Paul II thanked the Parisians for the way they had welcomed the young people. His address then turned to the hopes that he would kindle in Paris. "Too often the young fall victim to lack of job security, to extreme poverty; their generation seeks with difficulty not only adequate living standards but something to live for and goals that will give some point to their generosity." His visit was to have a social purpose. Already the newspapers were printing headlines such as: "Together with thousands of young people, the Pope launches an attack on the wall of indifference."

Feeling the excitement of their final rehearsal, the young people could not help looking up into the

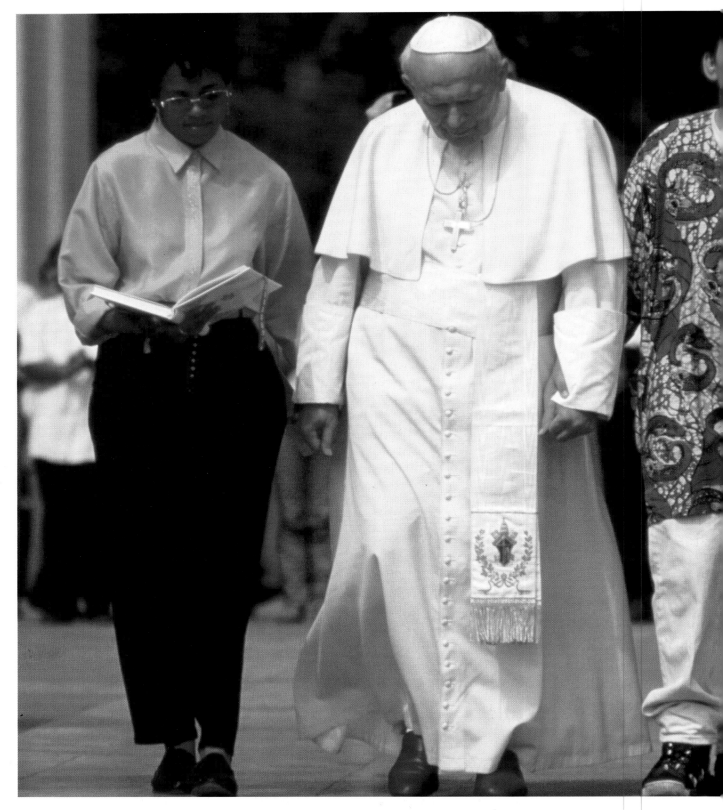

sky to try to see their idol. John Paul II was being carried by the air force and his aircraft would soon pass overhead. Discreetly, Geneviève Anthonioz-De Gaulle signalled to the producer to prompt the "children" in their piece. One hour later, a sizeable crowd had lined up behind the barriers. Suddenly, a ripple ran through the crowd. The popemobile was on its way. Standing up and holding the bar with his right hand, the Pope waved to the enthusiastic crowd. The vehicle came to a halt in the Pope greeted her and embraced her. With her at his side, he slowly walked towards the paving stone on which his friend Wresinski had had these words engraved: "Wherever people are condemned to live in a state of wretchedness, human rights are violated; to work together so that these rights are upheld is a sacred duty."

Ten young girls and boys, symbolizing the diversity of all the people of the world, came forward and, flanking the Pope, made their way with him to the tribune. Walking slowly, they went hand in hand. It was impossible to say who was moved the most: the young people or the older man. As she walked on the right-hand side of the Pope, an African teenager read to him a passage on courage and generosity. Slightly stooping, his head bent forward, John Paul II's thoughts were with his Polish friend whom he had supported in his winning battles. Father Wresinski had persuaded the government to institute a guaranteed minimum wage. He restored dignity to those who are excluded from an economic system on the downturn. In his tribute, John Paul II did not have time to mention all that his compatriot had undertaken. Watching the Pope leave the esplanade, the friends of Father Wresinski remembered the advice that he humorously gave to schoolchildren: "If you can't read, you'll always be the slaves of the well-off, of syndicates and of curates!" ■

123

the Place des Droits de l'Homme. John Paul II had come to pay tribute to Father Wresinski, founder of the humanitarian association ATD-Quart Monde (ATD Fourth World). As the association's president, Anthonioz-De Gaulle stepped forward,

Photographs Marc-Eric Gervais

◀ 50,000 young people gathered in the Champs-de-Mars,
August 21, 1997.

John Paul Two
we love you !

This was more than a cry from the heart; it was a real liberation. Up on the rostrum, a young Thai woman, a dark red shawl draped over her shoulders, fixed her cat-like gaze on the Pope. She delivered each syllable in a strong voice: "John Paul Two, we love you". This declaration was immediately taken up by the pilgrims, who started chanting it at the tops of their voices. Rosanne was sitting among them and she felt the tingle of gooseflesh. Rarely had she sensed such a collective wave of emotion.

They had all waited long enough! She had reached the Eiffel Tower at about 3 pm and volunteer stewards had shown her to one of the areas where there was still a little space. She had carefully picked her way through this multitude of young people. Some had been there since morning. She stepped over the sleeping bodies of those who, the night before, had followed up their religious meditation with a thorough tour of the nightclubs of Paris. Rosanne found a small patch of grass where she could sit down. She was slightly out of the way on the right-hand side of the esplanade but she could enjoy a little of the shade provided by the hundred-year-old plane trees that lined the walkways. She was, however, quite a distance from the podium from which the Pope was due to speak. To her, the stage seemed tiny. She could hardly make out the gigantic bronze figure of Christ that seemed to echo the Eiffel Tower. She really did not care at all about not being able to meet the Pope: all she wanted was to understand.

126 Looking about her, she spotted some young Spaniards who had organized drinking water and were passing it around, all in the middle of this joyful rowdiness. A group of bare-chested Germans were playing cards. Some girls were sitting cross-legged, reading. Others, sitting back to back, were writing postcards. Rosanne smiled inwardly at the sight of these young people sharing out tasks, just as her family did at home, then she carried on surveying the scene.

A youngster from Cameroon was blowing kisses to a Swedish girl. His envious friends looked around for other ways to do their bit for international understanding. Further off, an Italian girl, who had interrupted her holidays so as to come to Paris, was brushing her long hair. Looking at these people, Rosanne thought to herself that there really was no difference between Catholics and non-Catholics. For her, the image of religion as something that was fossilized in the past and out of step with the present evaporated. Just at that moment, Rosanne was part of their age group.

Photographs Marc-Eric Gervais

Various bands took the stage in succession. They expressed the cultural riches of the world and their performances, which were sometimes rewarded by salvos of applause, were relayed on a giant screen. Yet the crowd on the Champs-Élysées became slightly restless as they waited. Suddenly, Dee Dee Bridgewater, a black American singer with blonde hair, grabbed the microphone. Through loudspeakers the crowd, suddenly stock still, was told that it was going to get the breath of air it had been waiting for. The singer hardly had the chance to get to the end of the first line of "Happy Day" than the audience of half a million metamorphosed into half a million voluntary choristers.

Nuns, teenagers from the outskirts of Boston, students from The Hague, young au pair girls, country vicars – all melded into a single choir as they sang the greatest open-air gospel in the world. This was Harlem-on-Seine. Rosanne, who had merely come to see, felt a quiver run through her body. A tomboyish girl from Rotterdam took her by the sleeve and led her into this whirlpool of faith. People were dancing the sega and the madison, the twist and the rock and roll. Rosanne was bathed in sweat. Overdraft problems evaporated; the chore of shopping went up in smoke; the piles of ironing that awaited her disappeared. She felt vibrant from the depths of her soul. If only her husband could see her! Just thinking about it she threw back her hair and danced all the more energetically. She had her arms round the shoulders of a student girl from Prague when a shout of joy drowned out the singer and her band.

Instinctively, everyone turned towards the gangway. People were waving flags in all directions. Nuns fell to their knees. Priests prayed. Thousands of white scarves fluttered on a unprecedented breeze of love. Girls hoisted on the shoulders of boys waved their arms in the air, yelling. They made the sign of victory in the sky. Some silently wept. Rosanne was dazed by so much fervour; before her very eyes, the Pope had just arrived.

128

Everyone in the crowd, was listening intently to hear the Holy Father's message. Brief pauses punctuated his speech. The heat made it taxing for him to read in different languages. The Bishop of Rome spoke to the crowd for over an hour. He seemed tired. Rosanne closed her eyes the better to understand what she was hearing. For her, all this was so new: the enthusiasm whipped up by Dee Dee Bridgewater, the joy at the Pope's arrival, and that amazing slogan: "John Paul Two, we love you!". Why did they love this man so much?

Like most French people, Rosanne had a somewhat negative attitude towards him. On certain issues, such as abortion and the use of contraceptives, she found him backward-looking. As to the message that he had been developing for 20 years, she openly admitted that she had never really taken it in. For her, this was an opportunity to find out more. On her right, the screen relayed the picture of the elderly man. He seemed so full of goodwill. She was caught up in the emotional charge that electrified the Champ-de-Mars. She

applauded when he provoked a response from the crowd with words that touched her heart: "When people are suffering, when they are humiliated by poverty or injustice, and when they are deprived of their rights, go to their aid." Rosanne decided to hear him out.

She liked the maturity shown by these youngsters, who had a lot to say in response to what they heard. She was amazed that the political tone of the message captivated these young people, who showed no great interest in the political life of their respective countries. She was quite bowled over when they gave the Pope a standing ovation as he asked of them: "Let us pray for those young people who have neither the possibility nor the means to live with dignity, nor the opportunity of the education that is necessary for their human and spiritual development, be it because of poverty, war, or illness." On the rostrum Monsignor Dubost, the organiser of this World Youth Day, was surveying the crowd with open joy. Even he was stunned by the success of these Days.

So many people had repeatedly told him that the project would never get off the ground that he had sometimes had second thoughts. But now, at the height of summer, in the stifling heat and with drinking water at a premium, here were 500,000 people, camped out in the dust and often not very comfortably seated. Who would have dare believe that 500,000 "right-minded people" would be spellbound by a philosophical discourse? The stakes were high and he had taken an enormous risk. The press had even got him to admit that the Pope could not now rally 100,000 people. What a turn-up for the books! On the other hand, it had to be said that, for many, what was happening just then was a little surreal.

In an age when the briefest political speeches are often the best, the Pope succeeded in putting over a message that was not the most accessible. He had started off with the symbolism of the washing of the feet and had many times quoted from the Gospels: words like these stood no chance of being broadcast during prime viewing or listening time. But no-one got up and left! Although his speech was a little hesitant and was hampered by a slight accent, he was applauded as no political leader in Paris would ever be. And the Holy Father could not have been less like a popular politician. In a society that values form over content and in which the cult of the body over that of the soul was developing, his outward appearance counted against him. John Paul II was a million miles away from the kind of global marketing strategy that influences people's voting habits today. At a time when the Church was experimenting with publicity, Biblical references were still difficult to package, even when reduced to their simplest format. Just such an example is "Love your enemies". Yet here were 500,000 people who were united in their reaction to this dictum and applauding it.

Sitting in the shadow of the Eiffel Tower, her arms hugging her legs, Rosanne pursued her train of thought. Gradually she was coming to understand

the impact that this man and his message were having on the crowds. She was comparing what she was hearing here with various political speeches of the last few years. She had the feeling that the Pope was heard because his message was different. He did not promise a brighter future only for that future to disappoint. He did not explain today what could not be tomorrow. He did not waver in the face of the smallest shift of opinion on the part of a changeable society. On the contrary, in the domain of personal life, John Paul II refused to fall into step with today's women, who were in control of their bodies and of their potential to bear children. Now, in that crowd there were hundreds of thousands of women, enthusiastic and each one as modern, feminine and independent as the next. They insisted on the freedom to give birth when they wanted to. And yet, they literally sanctified this man who refused to put aside his beliefs for the sake of appearing to move with the times. Even more difficult to understand, the Pope was urging these young people to put their hearts

into an endeavour that, in a media-based society that values only that which is visible, would be scarcely perceptible.

Through this subtle form of infatuation, he was encouraging them to take responsibility for themselves in an age when the state is expected to provide. Going even further, the Holy Father was calling for a collegiate responsibility that would challenge secular dogmas that govern the workplace or that promote the primacy of the individual over group enterprise.

Now, Rosanne was sure that she had understood. He would restore hope and renew courage. He was unifying, for the greater good of mankind. He did not divide but he welcomed all to him without distinction. This – a message of truth and optimism – is what young people were looking for. As she left the Champ-de-Mars she smiled as the Holy Father ended on a humorous note. Knowing the attractions of Paris, the Pope flashed a smile as he entreated the young men and women to "Sleep well": whether this was a piece of advice or a final injunction was impossible to say. Rosanne was anxious to tell her husband what she had done, seen, and heard.

At home, Michel was watching the news on the television when a whirlwind burst in on him. Without giving him the chance to react, the young woman told him about all the feelings that had electrified her that day. Having experienced this living faith, she described to him the stuff that today's Catholics are made of. She wanted to share, and expected him to share, her enthusiasm. But already she came up against his reserve. Did she not have the right to find out about things and to ask questions.

Seeing so much fire in her, Michel promised to accompany her to Longchamp. He would probably find it quite fun: for him, religion stopped at buying weekly instalments of *The Bible on Video*, which fascinated his eleven-year-old son. Even though it was late, Rosanne got on the phone to rally their friends to a party that a million people were avidly looking forward to.

■

▲ The young people attended the churches of Paris, each church catering for a particular community.

▼ John Paul II in Notre Dame Cathedral, August 22, 1997.

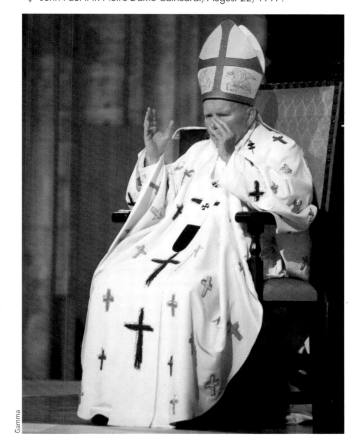

Gamma

As he walked into his usual café, Michel wondered whether he were dreaming. For once, everyone in there was not discussing football. That morning of Friday, August 22, the topic of conversation was John Paul II and the smiles on the faces of the young. It was the talk of the town. Everyone aired their opinion about this youth that was supposed to be "lost" and that seemed to bring to the adult world a renewed zest for life. For once, Jean-Marie, the barman, was at a loss to find anyone with whom to share his usual inflammatory racist remarks. He even held back from any unseemly comment when one of his customers quoted a passage from *Le Parisien*: "We refuse to see poverty destroy humanity. To work together so that human rights are upheld is a sacred duty." With these words, the Pope had brought in focus the historical tradition of a country that, with his visit, was at the centre of the world – Michel and his friends felt pleased about that.

A few yards away, the atmosphere was even more highly charged. By 9 am a party atmosphere had already broken out. At the church of Auteuil, tucked away in an upmarket area of Paris, some young Asian participants in World Youth Day were enjoying themselves to the full. Koreans and Taiwanese were greeting Vietnamese Catholics from every country. They had just attended a communal Mass. They were happy to be spending the day together and to chat about their families. Some had gathered in the sacristy to watch a re-run transmission of the Pope's beatification of Frédéric Ozanam, founder of the Society of St Vincent de Paul, at the cathedral of Notre Dame. Inside the cathedral, a festive atmosphere reigned. Thousands of the faithful were vigorously waving white handkerchiefs to bid John Paul II farewell as he left for Evry.

Later, in the helicopter that was bringing him back to Paris, the Pope became aware of the opprobrium that his visit was attracting. He was under attack from those who criticized him for holding a gathering on St Bartholomew's night. He could not suppress a sigh. Neither he nor anyone else could have foreseen that the Longchamp evening would coincide with the 428th anniversary of that horrific massacre, which normally no-one commemorated.

He also keenly felt the criticism with which his wish to visit the tomb of Father Lejeune had been met. It was true that the Holy Father felt close to the man who had discovered trisomy-21, the chromosomal abnormality most usually responsible for Down's Syndrome; but he also founded the association "*Laissez-les vivre*" (Let them live). He had admired his self-sacrifice for the sake of these sick children and the help he gave to families affected by this tragedy. Yet, the Bishop of Rome had no time for the extremist attitude of pro-life campaigners on the American model who, through their lack of moderation, distanced themselves from faith. Because, for him, faith is fundamentally non-violent.

Mopping his brow, he asked himself how many times he had expressed his opposition to abortion and, alongside this, how many times he had condemned all acts of violence. He loathed abortion, which seemed to him to equal a rejection of Jesus. "God is life." But he also considered that abortion was an unacceptable negation of womanhood. Sometimes, he railed against those who criticized him for his dogmatic approach. They believed that he had no idea what a woman who has been forced to these limits feels for years afterwards. But he did understand. One day, he had even implored: "Do everything you can so that she doesn't have to go through that." Of course, it was up to each woman to follow her own conscience in solving this problem. How many times had he said that he understood that a woman could make this choice and that God would forgive. But, seeing the Virgin Mary in every woman, John Paul II would have given all, even his own life, to save a woman from this irreversible trauma.

That day, August 23, the Pope no longer knew what to do to make himself heard. Yesterday morning, he had been speaking out for human rights and in the afternoon he had exhorted the young to unite against exclusion. That morning he had paid tribute to the courage of lay people such as Ozanam. At Evry he had heard every confession and had had the satisfaction of furthering the cause of greater understanding between all religions. In an hour, he was due to address the bishops, ordering them to ask the forgiveness of French Jews, before the end of September, for the Church's unforgivable silence during World War II. What more could he do? In that late afternoon, the Holy Father felt that he was spending all his time apologizing. As he gazed out of the helicopter window, he said to himself: "Perhaps that is how it should be."

Then the sound of the helicopter blades made him drowsy. While others in Paris were deep in thought, prayer and meditation, John Paul II dozed for a short while. ∎

Photographs Marc-Eric Gervais

141

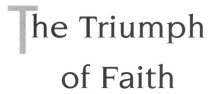

The Triumph
of Faith

Moving in a continuous flow, hundreds of thousands of pilgrims were flocking through the gates of Longchamp racecourse, set within expanse of greenery that stretches out on the west side of Paris. That Saturday, August 23, 1997 the youth of the world had answered the call of John Paul II: they were to gather for an evening meeting, and it would be followed by the largest Mass ever celebrated in the history of France. The crowd was getting larger all the time, and the participants felt that this could almost be St Peter's Square, in Rome: things had been arranged so that the Pope might feel at home.

From the vantage point of the press box, Jean-Marie Duthilleul, a planner with the French railway board, looked out over millions of dots of colour that filled the central arena. The 47-year-old graduate of a prestigious engineering college was smiling to himself. In a few minutes, the bet would be won. He thought back to the day when, out of friendship for Monsignor Dubost, he had replied: "Yes, that's possible." Unpaid, he had drawn up a plan for the site and set up the altar from which the Pope would say Mass. Mindful of the frail health of this elderly man, he had modelled the site on the exact proportions of St Peter's Square. The altar here in Paris was therefore set at an identical height to the balcony that was so familiar to the Vicar of Christ. The areas that the pilgrims were to occupy were divided by wide transverse gangways of the same proportions as those dictated by

Marc-Eric Gervais

142

Ettore Malanca

Vatican protocol. This was the work of a true professional. Yet, much spleen had been vented against this anonymous gift of skill by a profession that considered that architecture was under no obligation to carry out acts of charity for the Church.

A world away from this commercial mindset, which belonged to another age, Rosanne, Michel and their friends were filing into the area adjacent to the official rostrum. For two hours, guests and numerous men of the cloth had been making their way into the VIP area. Michel noticed that a few of the priests were positioned with their backs turned to the stage. A slight unevenness in the drape of their albs betrayed the presence of the standard-issue .357 Magnum that each was carrying. Maximum security had been laid on. There were fears of a shooting incident, which would have given publicity to extremist groups worldwide. The rostrum was surrounded by 250 police officers and 1500 secret service agents were mingling in the

143

Photographs Marc-Eric Gervais

crowd. Nothing, save perhaps for their greater reserve, made them stand out from the young, when an explosion of joy greeted the announcement that a meal was about to be distributed: 10,000 volunteers, girls and boys, were already briskly handing it out.

It was just after 6 pm. The young people were famished. That same morning, a large number of them had formed a gigantic chain of fraternity. Along 22 miles of boulevards, 300,0000 pilgrims had joined hands as the church bells of Paris rang out. Facing out from the capital to symbolize their opening out to the world, these youngsters were roused from their thoughts with an "Ola" delivered by the Brazilians. This could have been Rio, at the heart of the samba. At the signal, the disciplined crowd took less than five minutes to clear this great circle of streets, leaving them free for motorists. Then, their rucksacks on their backs and their duvets slung over their shoulders, they quietly made their way to Longchamp.

Just then, nothing would have kept these young people from their feast. Like everyone else, Michel, Rosanne and their friends were tucking into refreshments, seated on the grass. Between mouthfuls of chicken, these new arrivals on the path of faith were lavish in their praise for an organisation that seemed to them to be perfect. A commercial firm had pulled off a feat of organization: 1000 members of staff were available to see that everyone had everything that they needed. For them, "Operation World Youth Day" had only just begun. They would be on voluntary duty all through the night, serving breakfast next morning and then a meal after Mass. The largest party of dinner guests in the history of Christianity had taken on pharaonic proportions. Those responsible for laying on this mass meal had had the sense to keep it to a human scale. Food was not handed out on an assembly line. Sitting in circles, the young were enjoying their refreshments in groups of six. There was a convivial atmosphere, almost a family ambience. These youngsters were

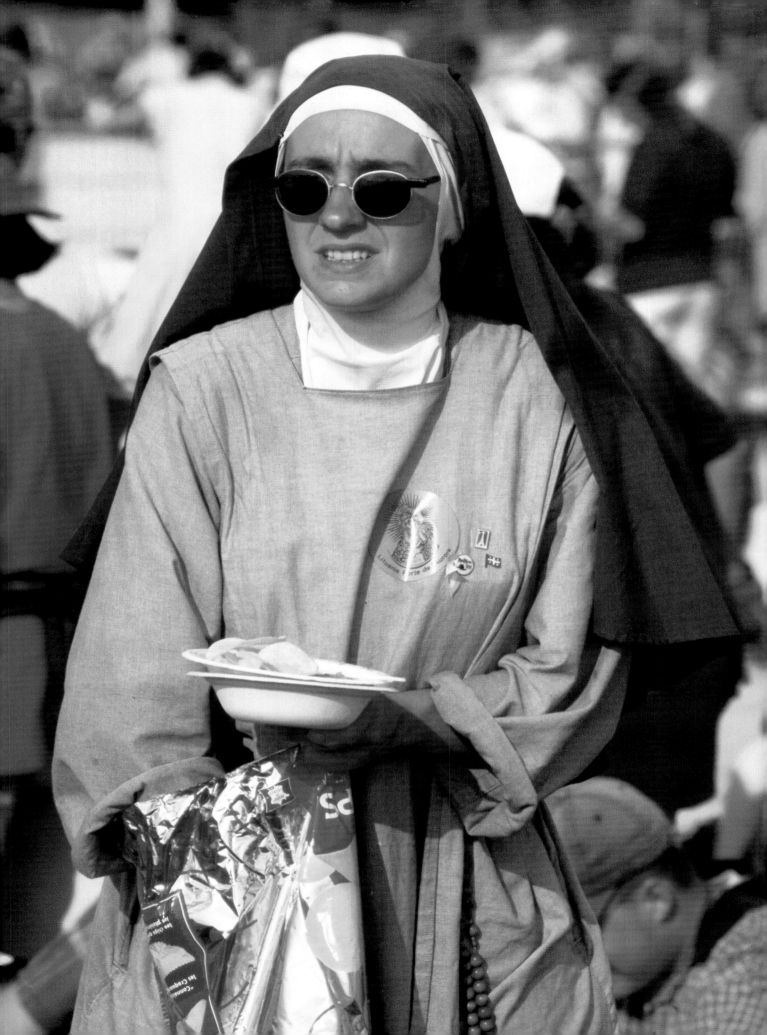

far away from their families, and the Church had decided to take good care of them. The culinary expertise of France went down well with these young foreigners.

Now, Longchamp was packed out. Several times, Monsignor Dubost asked the pilgrims to move closer together so that those who were still waiting outside could come in. The youngsters paid scant attention to the request. They were too busy settling down comfortably for this festive night. Rosanne and her friends, who had not envisaged spending the night there, made room for some new arrivals. They were priests from the Wallis and Futuna Islands, a territory of France in the south western Pacific. Rosanne's party immediately began chatting to these compatriots from the other side of the world. Here were people with completely different ideas about life. But the conversation was friendly. The non-religious people were glad to be able to broach subjects that weighed on their minds, and the religious people were delighted to welcome non-believers who had come and who had seen. Gilles, the godfather of Michel's daughter, brought up the well-worn issue of the use of contraceptives and the ravages of AIDS. Father Alain Gérard, who had worked as a priest in Africa, gave a straight answer. Choosing his words carefully so as not to be misunderstood, he explained the Church's position and his own views, which had grown out of his experience. To the disbelief of those to whom he was speaking, he summed up his thoughts on the issue by quoting the Holy Father: "Love your life and the life of your partner. Love is not worth dying for."

Then, Father Gérard responded to a suggestion that whatever the Pope had to say was centred around morals. He simply stated that fewer than ten per cent of John Paul II's writings and statements were to do with personal life. A wily psychologist, the priest in turn asked them a question on the issue of faithfulness. There was no argument. The women said that they had never been cheated on. Neither had Michel and Gilles.

Photographs Marc-Eric Gervais

Ettore Malanca

On this, they were in complete agreement with the words of the Holy Father. Suddenly, and for no particular reason, the Pope seemed to them to be less backward-thinking. They had come to see. They were not going to be disappointed.

When she heard cheering rise up from the back of the racecourse, Annie, an army nurse, breathed a sigh of relief. He was on his way and that would be

a relief to those suffering from the heat. The efforts of the Korean conductor Myung Whun Chung had provided some distraction, but many young people were feeling faint. In the last hour, Annie and her team had come to the aid of almost a hundred cases. The sun was quickly going down. Its fiery rays bathed the popemobile in a rare luminosity. "I Believe", the song that Dee Dee Bridgewater had written and dedicated to the Pope, floated on to

the air. To exuberant shouts and thunderous applause, John Paul II was approaching the altar. As he raised his arms, night suddenly fell. The timing was perfect. Michel and Gilles glanced at each other. They were impressed.

The crowd, as one, watched intently as the Pope took his place beneath the huge cross. Lit with spotlights, it seemed to bear down on him. John Paul II seemed so humble and so frail, so much an ordinary mortal. Arc lights, forming gigantic Gothic vaults, played in the sky above. Rosanne and her friends could have been in St Peter's Basilica. Here, at the very heart of religion, were 700,000 people. Now, the Holy Father could set rolling the greatest baptismal night of the late 20th century.

The Bishop of Rome immediately infused his service with his love for mankind. Speaking from the heart, he addressed the Protestant community in particular. Many of those who were standing on the pale wooden stage were looking for a sign from the Roman Catholic Church that would indicate its new-found universality: "Certain Christians have committed acts that the Gospel condemns." On St Bartholomew's night, one man was speaking out against all holocausts.

His words were greeted by an ovation. Catholicism was taking on yet another humanist dimension, one that was very far away from idolatry. One faith drew the world to this man who had been the focus of so much criticism for his views on personal life and yet had been so close to people's everyday expectations. A light refreshing wind got up and the Pope went on: "Do not lose courage. Keep working for reconciliation and peace."

He called for unity between all religions. "Who could be against that?" asked Michel as he turned to Gilles. Without missing a beat, his friend replied with a smile: "You're right. No-one. And who else would say that?" Deep down, Gilles, who through circumstance had been deprived of the oppportunity to continue his education, was moved by the things the Pope had said since his arrival in Paris. He felt grateful to him for having reiterated that education is everyone's just due and that every individual has the right to make the best of their life. Gilles's concerns were naturally more social than spiritual. But, just then, he was wondering whether religion was not part of an indivisible whole that was the framework for a certain approach to life.

Later, all eyes were on the central gangway. The procession of new converts was underway. The press caught the solemn faces of ten youngsters and their godparents as they approached the altar. Representing the five continents, they had chosen to be baptized that evening, by the Pope.

Bringing up the rear, Arnaud, a young sailor of 24, was visibly overcome with emotion. At his side, a young Kenyan woman of noble demeanour was trying to put to the back of her mind the sufferings of her community, that in that late summer was being torn apart by bloody murders. At the very moment when Britain was handing Hong Kong over to the People's Republic of China, here was a young man from the Wanchai district, whom the universal Church was leading to baptism. His presence served as a reminder to all of the persecution of the Tibetan people and the sufferings of Chinese Catholics who, threatened with imprisonment, were forced to worship in the utmost secrecy.

Marc-Eric Gervais

152

There was absolute silence. The pilgrims were holding their breath. No-one wanted to spoil the initiation ceremony of these ten children of God. No orders had been given but, with this spontaneous sense of discipline, the youth of the world gave adults a demonstration of how to show respect. Standing stock still, Rosanne took her husband's hand. By her side, her eyes focused on the stage, Christine, Gilles's wife, was praying. The Pope looked radiant. Monsignor Lustiger presented the young people to him. This was no mere show: they were thirsting for faith. One by one they came before the Vicar of Christ to receive the sacrament of baptism. The Pope rose to his feet. With his right hand he took up a silver cup representing the shell of St James of Compostela. The converts knelt and received the holy water, symbol of purification. Each person's face seemed to be bathed in the love of life.

Then it was the turn of Jacqueline Mwangi, a girl from Mombasa. The Pope fixed her with a solemn

gaze. He knew that the part of Africa that she came from had known many a scourge. This land of hope for Catholics was ravaged by corruption, poverty, civil war and AIDS. Though it was a playground for rich holidaymakers, Kenya had not escaped. On that St Bartholomew's night, near the upmarket districts of the capital, John Paul II had mustered all the love that the world had to give.

As he met those eyes, filled with love, the Holy Father's gaze became downcast. Then, he remembered a meeting that he had had with Nafis Sadik. On March 18, 1994, he had given an informal audience to this delegate from the United Nations. Two different viewpoints on birth control had come face to face. As far as the head of the universal Church was concerned, there were no rights nor needs for individuals; there were only rights and needs for couples. The United Nations, which represented the different cultures of six thousand million people, was pleading for the rights of women and the establishment of real sexual equality. This standpoint was more than a concession to the feminist lobby. It was the result of a serious issue in Third World countries – the problem of legal rape of a wife by her husband, lord and master.

How many women in that predicament would have wanted to be able to refuse their husbands? How could they prevent the arrival of another child, whom they could not feed? Finding no way out of the problem, many of them overrode their maternal instinct. They could not bear to think that the child might die of hunger or disease. How could they face giving birth only to hand the child over to some institution, assuming that that were possible? For them, was not the crime more frightful and the trauma even more unbearable? They had no option but to use their own methods to terminate a pregnancy. Every year, 200,000 of them died from backstreet abortions, the abortions of shame.

Taking Jacqueline's hand, John Paul II came back to the question that he had put to the representative of the United Nations: "Do you not think that it is the fault of women if men behave irresponsibly?" Straightaway he – who was usually so warm-hearted – had taken himself to task for this lack of compassion. Later on, at a remove from the fury that inexorably followed that question, he explained that he had been thinking of Western society, where generally "women were perfectly capable of avoiding sexual relations if they so wished". In fact, he had taken some of the credit for the repressive evolution of anti-rape legislation. A large number of developed countries, including the United States, justly punish all sexual acts committed without consent whether within or outside marriage and by whoever they are committed. The Pope approved of this situation, and many women would be relieved to learn of it.

This pope simply did not know how to explain his feelings of pain when men, unable to distinguish freedom from immorality, subject women to acts

that compromise their dignity. And that, John Paul II will never bring himself to accept. He sincerely wanted women to step out of the shadows into which history has pushed them since the beginning of time.

In receiving all these young people under the starry Longchamp sky, he was thinking of their future. He saw these children of God who wholeheartedly pledged themselves to him. The Pope wanted the best for them – a home, a family and children – and, for their happiness, adequately paid work for the sake of their dignity and fulfilment. As if it could read his thoughts, the crowd was waiting. With the utmost love, he poured the water over the young woman's face. Seven hundred thousand people, including Rosanne and Christine, crossed themselves. They were reborn into faith. Gilles was deep in thought. Michel was thinking of his two children. He missed them.

In the mass emotion of this crowd, lit by thousands of candles, Michel suddenly thought about that

153

child who would have reached his 20th year on the feast day of the Virgin Mary. Twenty years had gone by since a look had changed the lives of two adolescents. Gazing into the distance, he remembered.

They would love one another for eternity: of that they were quite certain. There followed a night of love. They went further than they had ever done before. In Rosanne's house, there was ill feeling between a father who was losing his daughter and the man who was "stealing" her from him. When the suspicion that she was pregnant gave way to certain knowledge, she dared not mention it to her family. After a tearful night, they had decided not to keep the baby. What else could they do? They had been seeing one another for only two months. At that particular time in their young lives, they could not know that they would eventually get married and that children who were very much wanted would arrive.

They did not know how their feelings would develop. They were so much at a loss to know what to do in this predicament that Michel went to see his father and told him about this lapse in his conduct. The reception was glacial. His father enquired what decision the young woman had come to. He made no comment, promised to take care of everything and turned on his heel. Michel remembered what he had said: "A lifetime will not be long enough to forget. Do all you can so that this woman overcomes this ordeal that will be with her for ever." They never spoke about it again.

In the middle of hundreds of thousands of little flames that shone like rays of truth, Michel fixed his gaze on the altar. He wanted to go up and see this pope, and to tell him about his pain. He so wanted to tell him that he did not believe in "abortion on demand". He wanted John Paul II to know that, for all the times that he severely labelled abortion "a crime against humanity", old wounds reopened and became more difficult to heal. As if the Pope had guessed the needs of this lost man, a strong

voice spoke of hope: "The word of God transforms the life of those who allow it in, for it is the staff of faith and the benchmark of action. In order to respect fundamental values, Christians will also experience pain in their life; pain caused by moral choices that are at odds with the ways of the world and that are therefore sometimes heroic."

While a sublime Magnificat was being sung, the youth of the world bade the Holy Father farewell. Thousands of brightly coloured scarves fluttered in the darkness of the night. Rosanne took her husband's hand. As the music, indescribably beautiful, rose up into the sky, they felt closer to one another than ever.

Journalists and guests were trickling away from Longchamp. However, the empty press box was resounding to singing that was coming from the esplanade. The young people were in no mood to go to sleep. After quite a lengthy baptismal ceremony, they needed to unwind. People of all

155

158

nationalities mingled. Language barriers collapsed spontaneously. Just a wink or a laugh, and people understood. Under the eyes of the exhausted volunteers, a group from Madrid broke into a very un-Catholic macarena. They were swiftly joined by some Koreans who, quite unexpectedly, shouted out in Spanish the words of the song. The dancing, initiated by some 15 young men, spread throughout the whole assembly. Tens of thousands of people, grouped in hundreds of rows, stretched out their arms and moved to the same beat.

That night there was great pleasure in just being together. Two Polish girls made a striking contrast with two Chileans who, without warning, had switched from the macarena to the lambada. In this party atmosphere, the teenagers from Kraków could forget about the nights that they had spent working to scrape together the hundreds of dollars needed to make the journey. That night they felt too happy to think of the familiar work routine that awaited them on their return. Very many of them would have to repay the spare time they had taken so as to

come to Paris to join the school of faith. Not one would have wanted to miss this opportunity to hear in the flesh a teacher who put so much talent and so much heart into the will to change life. Later, the atmosphere was calmer. The strains of a guitar could be heard in the distance. Only the camp fires and the crackle of wood were missing. Many were speaking in a whisper so as not to disturb those few souls who wanted to sleep. Catholic and proud of it, they wanted to watch the sunrise together. It would not be long before the Pope would be there to celebrate the largest Mass in history.

That Sunday, 24 August 1997, the thermometer was already showing 82°F when Pope John Paul II made his entrance to Longchamp racecourse. So enthusiastic was the ovation that it took him by surprise. The Bishop of Rome looked worn out but he could not help smiling. He was being acclaimed by 1,150,000 people: that was 500,000 more than the evening before! Monsignor Lustiger, beside him in the popemobile, was jubilant. Something had definitely changed in France.

Marc-Eric Gervais

The evening before, the Holy Father had concentrated on reconciliation and unity between all religions. That day, he would speak of the road to faith. Announcing that Saint Theresa of Lisieux was to be proclaimed a Doctor of the Church, he wanted to instil in the young the habit of daily worship: "It is better to spend a little time on religion every day than a lot of time intermittently." For that reason, he felt close to Saint Theresa who, long before he did, had devoted her faith to the service of love of her neighbour.

Born in 1873, Theresa dreamed of only one thing: to enter the Carmelite convent on Christmas night. But she was only 14 years old. The Church authorities in Lisieux thus refused to grant this slip of a girl the right to become a nun. She was extremely headstrong, however, and she set off for Rome.

Joining a group of pilgrims from the diocese of Coutances, she spotted the opportunity of a lifetime when Pope Leo XIII granted a public audience on November 20, 1887. Not fully aware of what she was doing, she went and stood squarely before the Pope and said to him: "Your Holiness, I have a great favour to ask of you." The youngster explained to him that she had not been allowed to join a Carmelite convent. Taken aback by such audacity, Leon XIII riposted: "You will be admitted if the Good Lord wishes it."

A journalist who was travelling with these pilgrims reported this incident. Between them Theresa and the press forced the Catholic authorities to yield. On April 9, 1888, she became a Carmelite nun and took the name Theresa of the Christ Child. The Joan of Arc of faith, she fought valiantly for the cause of good. She died of tuberculosis at the age of 24, leaving on the table in her cell an exercise book in which she had recorded the pure happiness her spirituality her brought her. In her childish hand she had expressed her humility and her wholehearted desire to love God: "At the heart of the Church, my mother, I will be Love." Feeling her strength ebb away, Theresa marked the end of her life with these words: "In Heaven, I will spend my time doing good on Earth."

A century later, John Paul II raised the host, in spite of the pain that a hairline fracture in his right shoulder had been giving him off and on since 1993. Borne up by the words of the saint, the Pope overcame his weariness to deliver to the young people these words of wisdom: "Do not lose courage. Keep working for reconciliation and peace." He urged on the million pilgrims gathered before him: "Your path does not end here. Time does not stand still today. Go on. The Church puts its faith in you." All the pilgrims took communion. John Paul II promised to see them on the occasion of the next World Youth Day in Rome.

Finally, exhausted by this extraordinary week, he rose to his feet with difficulty and left to embark on other crusades. As if he had sensed the sadness of these million children who refused to let him go, he told them with a smile: "See you in the year 2000, God willing!"

∎

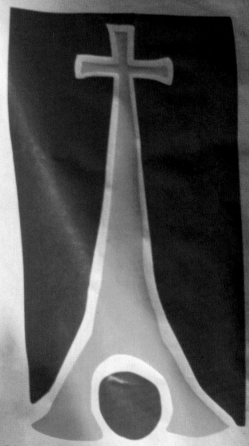

XIIèmes JOURNÉES MONDIALES
DE LA JEUNESSE
PARIS 1997

163

So Who Was John Paul II?

raging over the cost of the World Youth Day. A figure of 30,000,000 French Francs was quoted, though this actually boiled down to eight million Francs. Those 20,000,000 young people who had not paid for their stay became a bone of contention. In actual fact, the figure was actually less than 60,000 Francs. Raising these hollow issues was an attempt to play down the importance and success of this event.

The 12th World Youth Day had just drawn to a close. The evening before, Michel had watched the Pope's departure on television and had noticed the warmth with which the prime minister, Lionel Jospin, had treated him. Now the capital was silent. Parisians looked for the groups of people that had been around all through the previous week. They were aware that something was missing. A song, a smile – simply the young themselves. In spite of everything, controversy was

Like many others, Michel gave silent thanks to the French Church for having invested so much in the hopes and welfare of mankind. Unconsciously, he was asking himself what he would say to his children when the time came for them to ask: "Who was John Paul II, Daddy?"

He would tell them the story of an exceptional human being. He would tell them that his words were such a source of wisdom that he made of

them a gift to the world. He would tell them how their grandparents, their great grandparents and many other people had shared with him moments – often dramatic ones – in the history of the century in which they were born. He would go on to say that this man had come from a country that had known many troubles, that he had travelled all over the world, and that he brought hope. He would also tell them that their mother had met him, one day in Paris, and that she had believed in him.

What else would he say? That John Paul II had given his all to improve the lot of the ordinary men and women of the world. He would describe the Pope's anger in the face of wars, selfishness and suffering of any kind.

He would speak of his revolt against countries where 250 million children do not go to school but are put to work from the age of five. He would explain that the Pope's words were not always very well understood, and that the Holy Father knew and understood this. Michel would admit to his children that he did not believe in God but that this man had often moved him, sometimes influenced him and even made him laugh; that he did not walk on the water, nor perform miracles, but that Fidel Castro had celebrated Christmas at least once!

His children would undoubtedly find his answer too elaborate. But there is so much to say about humanity and goodness. He would explain to them that John Paul II had devoted his life to convincing human beings that they deserve more care and love than the 20th century has given them.

And Michel would add that this man was relying on children, like them, to usher in a new era in which men and women would at last find happiness.

Acknowledgments

The teams

        ELSA Editions
          -France-
          -United Kingdom-
          -United States-
        ELSA Ediciones
        ELSA Verlag

would like to thank all those who have contributed to the production of this book.

The author would like to thank His Holiness John Paul II and his office for having granted him an audience, and for authorizing the reproduction of one of his homilies on page 5. (Seventh Apostolic Voyage, Paris May 30, 1980.)

Bibliography

Works by Karol Wojtyla, before his pontificate.
Amour et responsabilité, Paris, Stock, 1978.
La Boutique de l'orfèvre, Paris, Cerf, 1979

Encyclicals.
*Redemptor hominis,*1979, Paris, Cerf, 1979.
Laborem exercens, 1980, Paris, Cerf, 1980.
Slavorum Apostoli, 1985, Médiaspaul, 1985.
Dominum et Vivificantem, 1986, Paris, le Centurion, 1986.
Redemptoris Mater, 1987, Paris, Le Centurion, 1987.
Veritatis splendor, 1993, Paris, Mame / Plon, 1993.

Bibliography
Malinski (Mieczyslaw), *Mon ami Karol Wojtyla*, Paris, Le Centurion, 1981
Gordon (Thomas) et Morgan Wittz (Max), *Dans les couloirs du Vatican*, Paris, Stock, 1983.
Chélini (Jean), *La vie quotidienne sous Jean-Paul II*, Paris, Hachette, 1985.
Decaux (Alain), *Le pape pèlerin, les voyages de Jean-Paul II*, Paris, Perrin 1986
Frossard (André), *Le monde de Jean-Paul II*, Paris, Fayard, 1991.
Frossard (André), *N'ayez pas peur !*, Paris, Fayard, 1991.
Dufourquet (Philippe), *Toi, je t'aime !* Paris, L'Ecrivain Public, 1992
Vircondelet (Alain), *Jean-Paul II*, Paris, Julliard, 1994
Bernstein (Carl), Politi (Marco), *Sa Sainteté*, Paris, Plon, 1996

Cover photographs:
Front cover : Gamma
Back cover : Arturo Mari, Gamma, Gamma, Marc-Eric Gervais

Printing Amilcare Pizzi - Milan
Dépôt légal : October 1998
(Printed in Italy)